The Sanitariums of Lake Geneva

Sonja Akright

Dedication

In honor of Dr. Oscar A. King and Dr. Mary E. Pogue

In memory of my friend Jim Davis

"Those who touch our lives, stay in our hearts forever."

And for my children, Megan Quinn, and Jackson Jayden, who
have lovingly endured my Sanitarium obsession and constant
"crazy" talk.

Acknowledgment

Words cannot adequately convey my gratitude and appreciation to Jessica Franzene Miller, who has not only listened to, championed, and promoted my zeal for the Sanitariums but without whom I would not have completed this journey.

My special thanks to Helen Brandt, Chris Brookes, Patrick Quinn, and Jim Davis for their invaluable historical insights, inspiration, and unwavering encouragement.

I wish to extend my deepest appreciation to the Geneva Lake Museum and the Lake Geneva Public Library for their invaluable support in providing countless hours of research. Having the platforms to present and promote this topic and the opportunity and space to curate an exhibit have been instrumental in bringing this project to fruition.

I am forever grateful to my family and friends for their support and to everyone who provided stories, memories, articles, pictures, relics, and the gift of their time. I am deeply thankful for your generosity and involvement.

Finally, my heartfelt appreciation and gratitude to Adam Colman Browne for generously gifting me a missing piece in my collection.

About the Author

Sonja Akright, a dedicated member of the Historic Preservation Commission of the City of Lake Geneva, works to safeguard and celebrate the community's historical heritage. Currently serving as a director on the board of the Geneva Lake Museum, she has curated an evocative exhibit exploring the fascinating history of the Sanitariums of Lake Geneva.

Growing up in Lake Geneva and her experiences working on the Lake Geneva Cruise Line gave her unique insights and inspiration to pursue her passion for historical knowledge of the area.

An engaging speaker and advocate for local history, Sonja has shared her insights at various venues, including the Geneva Lake Museum, the Lake Geneva Public Library, and in private settings. As the proprietor of Old Time Eyes, LLC, Sonja seamlessly combines her entrepreneurial spirit with her enthusiasm for history, significantly contributing to preserving and disseminating local narratives.

Sonja's journey as a representative, curator, presenter, and local historian reflects a deep-seated love for the stories woven into the fabric of Lake Geneva. Her work not only preserves the past but also brings it to life, enriching the understanding and appreciation of the community's unique legacy.

Preface

I wrote this book to evoke the forgotten stories that lie beneath layers of time and oblivion. It has been my quest to bring back to life narratives that have long been relegated to whispers and shadows.

As the storyteller of this historical journey, my purpose extends beyond the mere retelling of events. Through stories, anecdotes, and historical tidbits, I aspire to resurrect a past era, inviting you to step back in time and experience the history of the Sanitariums.

Furthermore, this is a call to action to appreciate, understand, and empathize with the past. It invites you- the reader, to join in the journey of discovery and become custodians of history. By understanding the purpose, you are encouraged to remember and actively preserve legacies that might otherwise fade away with time.

At its core, the pages unfold not solely documenting facts but as an empathetic exploration of lives lived within the Sanitarium's confines. It pays homage to the resilience of patients, the dedication of the staff, and the impact on the community.

Contents

Introduction

It all began with a single glimpse of a postcard of Oakwood Sanitarium, a breathtaking four-story brick structure that spoke to me in ways words could not describe. Questions provoked my curiosity, and I found myself craving the history of this architectural gem.

So, I started asking questions to locals, hoping to unearth the Sanitarium's past. But all I heard were murmurs—vague mentions of it being the "crazy house" and a long-forgotten relic, now lost to time.

What impacted me most was the void in locally recorded history—I could not get a clear picture of when it opened or what stories might be hidden within its walls. The mystery had piqued my interest, and the quest for knowledge began.

Armed with determination and tenacity, I started my research journey, diving into the world of the internet, state and local museums, historical societies, and libraries. It was like piecing together a puzzle where every scrap of information was a valuable clue.

As my journey brought me closer to my goal, I felt an urge to share this untold story with the world. I began to give presentations at the museum, joined forces with our local newspaper, and put out a call through them, asking for relics and stories related to the Sanitarium. Though modest, the response was like a flicker of curiosity that soon turned into a blaze.

People started sharing their stories, and I found myself holding relics that whispered tales of an era long gone. The presentations became a platform for locals to contribute their bits of history, and the more I spoke, the more the mysterious past of the Sanitarium unraveled before me. It felt like an unfolding mystery, with each revelation adding another layer to the narrative.

Motivated by this growing interest from others, I decided to take the story beyond the physical realm and created a dedicated Facebook page for sanitarium enthusiasts.

My passion spilled over—I would gladly take any ten-minute window to share the fascinating history I was uncovering. The pilgrimage to gather all this information and the relics was not a sprint but a marathon that spanned over 15 years.

The joy of discovering hidden bits and transforming them into a narrative made every moment of the pursuit worthwhile. I am inspired to keep unveiling the secrets of Oakwood Sanitarium and the Sanitariums of Lake Geneva.

The passage extends beyond the physical spaces, introducing you to the individuals and places that, even today, contribute to the revival of this history. The chapters unfold like a map, leading you through different eras, revealing the unsung heroes, and shedding light on each person's unique role in preserving the legacy.

By the end of this book, you will have gained knowledge and an enlightened understanding of the significance of the sanitariums of Lake Geneva.

Chapter 1: History of the Area

Figure 1: Lake Geneva

The protected Geneva Lake shore path, which today allows one to walk around the entire lake at the water's edge, traces its origins to an ancient Indian trail. This trail was later frequented by tradesmen and domestic workers serving the region's wealthy estates.

Approximately 18,000 years ago, as a glacier retreated northward, it sculpted the landscape and formed Geneva Lake, leaving behind a moraine of rolling hills. Originally named Kish-Way-Kee-Tow by the Potawatamie Indians who inhabited the region in the 1600s, 'Kishwauketoe' translates loosely to "Lake of the Sparkling Water."

The lake is fed entirely by underground springs and has no surface inlets. The only outlet, the White River, in the City of Lake Geneva, feeds into the Fox, Illinois, and Mississippi Rivers.

Natives built effigy mounds, fished, and hunted the land, skillfully utilizing the abundant wildlife and flourishing forests.

The area remained undiscovered by white settlers until 1831 when a party traveling with a family named Kinzie between Fort Dearborn in Chicago and Fort Winnebago near Portage, WI, first documented the lake.

By 1836, a dispute had arisen over the rights to the water power and dam site at the outlet of Geneva Lake into the White River. This conflict pitted John Brink, the government surveyor, against Christopher Payne, a frontiersman famous as Geneva's first settler. There were grist and sawmills built in a battle to settle ownership. The dispute was settled when Brink's group gathered $2,000 and paid off Payne's group.

Dr. Philip Maxwell played a pivotal role in securing funds, becoming one of the original six owners of Geneva. The town of Geneva was chartered and structured in 1837. When the town plat was complete, one broad tree-lined street was named in his honor. At about the same time, Chicago's Maxwell Street, now famous as a trader's paradise, was also named after Dr. Maxwell.

The area became a beacon of promise, attracting pioneers with dreams of a new life. In 1839, the Federal Government Land Office confirmed land sales at a remarkably affordable $1.25 per acre, and an influx of immigrant settlers surged into Geneva.

This wave of newcomers embarked on a harrowing journey, navigating steamboats and sailing ships through the vast Great Lakes.

By 1840, the landscape of Geneva had undergone a remarkable metamorphosis. In addition to the natural beauty of Geneva Lake, the cityscape boasted two hotels, two general stores, three churches, and even a distillery, signifying progress against the backdrop of mills, cabins, and houses that had taken root.

In 1844, the town of Geneva became an incorporated village. However, in 1882, the Post Office's name changed from "Geneva" to "Lake Geneva" just four years before becoming incorporated as a city. In the past, the beautiful lake played a stealthy role as a reverse route for escaped slaves before the Civil War rocked the nation from Southern Illinois and Eastern Kentucky.

It was a hidden pathway leading to the Great Lake ports, offering a chance at freedom. Fast forward to the aftermath of the war, a remarkable transformation occurred. Geneva Lake became more than a body of water; it was a refuge, a sanctuary of hope for those who dared to dream of an unshackled life. The shores harbored hushed tales of the brave souls who navigated the perilous journey to freedom and their allies who protected them.

Post-Civil War, Geneva Lake became a swanky retreat for wealthy families from Chicago. In the 1870s, men from Chicago came here to hunt, fish, and seek solace. Their love of the area convinced them that Geneva Lake would be the ideal place to build a summer cottage.

The glittering appeal of this lakeside escape attracted notable figures such as Mary Todd Lincoln, along with prominent military leaders General William T. Sherman and General Philip Sheridan.

As this wave of affluence settled over Geneva, the construction of opulent mansions commenced, dotting the landscape like jewels, earning it the moniker the "Newport (RI) of the West."

The Chicago and Northwestern Railroad opened a line from Chicago to the Village of Geneva on July 6, 1871. This facilitated the commute between Chicago and Geneva, especially following the Chicago Fire.

The Chicago Fire, on October 8, 1871, was a paradigm shift that spurred many families to seek refuge in their Geneva Lake summer cottages, commuting via rail to their businesses in the city while Chicago got back on its feet.

However, these were not just ordinary cottages; they were grand mansions and estates that needed tending. The late 19th century saw the rise of conspicuous consumption among the elite. Wealthy families invested in luxurious properties, gardens, and leisure activities. This created a demand for specialized services and products tailored to maintaining and enhancing these lifestyles.

The emergence of the service industry catering to the maintenance of lavish mansions often required a large staff to maintain and manage these properties. Those hired to cater to these needs included housekeepers, gardeners, cooks, butlers, tutors, nannies, chauffeurs, and other domestic staff, parallel to existing enterprises like milling, furniture making, and typewriter manufacturing.

Geneva Lake's fame reached new heights with its thriving ice harvesting industry. Before the advent of modern refrigeration, ice was harvested from frozen lakes and rivers during winter months and stored in ice houses for use throughout the year. This industry boomed during the late 19th century, with ice being a vital commodity for preserving food and providing refrigeration for estates, hotels, and households. The clear ice was in high demand, and thanks to the arrival of the railroad, tons of Geneva Lake ice were shipped annually to the Chicago market.

Over time, Geneva Lake became synonymous with luxury and leisure, with prominent families like Maytag, Swift, Schwinn, and Wrigley establishing summer estates along its shores.

It became a tradition that women and children would spend their summer there while working men shuttled back and forth on the train, cementing Geneva Lake as the go-to getaway for affluent Chicagoans.

The rich history of Geneva Lake is a tale of opulence, industry, and unexpected twists shaped by the ebb and flow of time, revealing the spirit of a community bound to the ever-changing currents of history, whispering its incredible saga to those who listen.

Chapter 2: Oakwood Sanitarium (1885 – 1928)

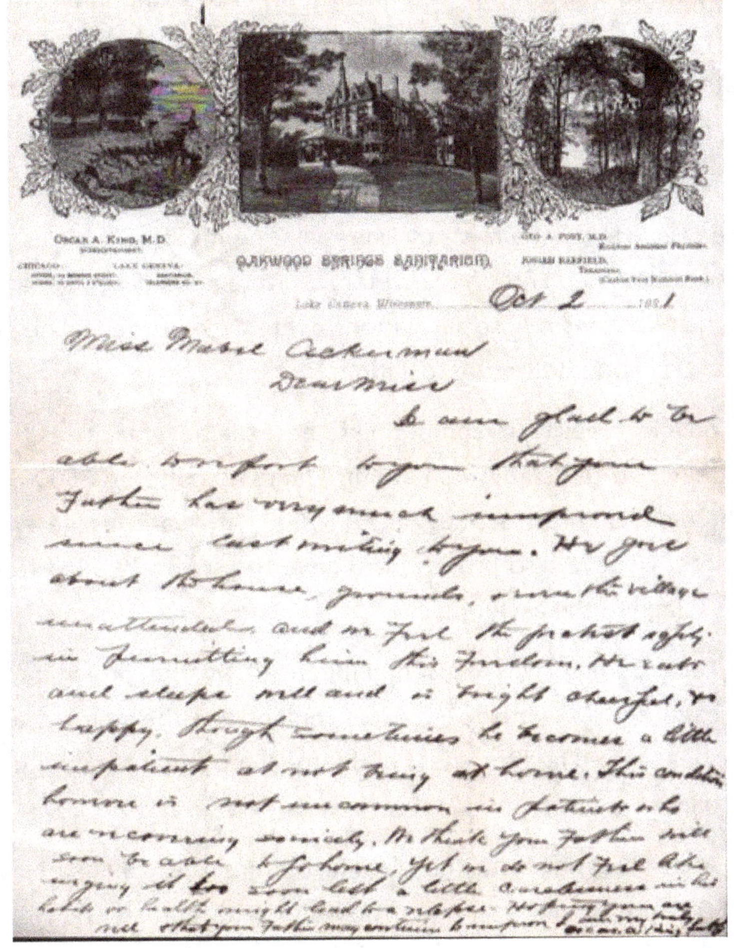

Figure 2: Oakwood Springs Sanitarium Letterhead

The nineteenth century was a period marked by rapid industrialization and urbanization; health concerns became increasingly paramount. People sought refuge from the stress and pollution of city life, and a new trend emerged: the establishment of sanitariums.

Dr. Oscar A. King was compelled to take on this undertaking since there was not a private institution of this kind in the west of Pennsylvania and New York, except for Batavia Place in Batavia, Illinois, which was limited to 2o patients and restricted to the admission of only ladies.

The new institution was founded in June of 1883 by Dr. King and Dr. Henry Palmer of Janesville, with the Articles of Association filed with the Secretary of State amending the name of the "Wisconsin Association for Private Care of the Insane" to the "Oakwood Retreat Association."

Several cities were competing to host the new facility as they endeavored to establish an asylum. Janesville offered $5000, as did Beloit. Lake Geneva suggested $1500 with water usage at no charge. Geneva also proposed to have the streets graded from the village to the asylum.

Lake Geneva was chosen, influenced by the proximity to Chicago and Milwaukee—the convenience of the railroad and the beauty and healthfulness of the fresh air climate and natural springs.

A city meeting with the planning committee would provide $2500 and a nominal charge for water with graded streets. In September of 1883, an immediate construction contract was initiated, with George H. Edbrook appointed as the architect and Waclav Horacek as the General Contractor, thanks to the acquisition of land from the Walter family -specifically, Joel

Clarke Walter and his wife, Ophelia Maxwell, who was the child of Dr. Philip and Jerusha Maxwell.

The projected completion date was set for March 1, 1884. However, as the date passed, a legal case followed, which eventually went to trial at the WI State Supreme Court under Oakwood Retreat Association v. Rathborne. The case raised concerns regarding deviations from the planned materials and the specifications, as well as the missed completion deadline. Despite delays, the building was finally erected over the winter of 1884-1885, leading to a favorable ruling for the Oakwood Retreat Association in the January term of 1886.

In 1885, Dr. King enlisted artist John Bullock to paint a series of views to have wood engravings made from them, illustrating the scenery of Lake Geneva, and the Sanitarium was advertised in the Lake Geneva Herald. The images were used in several medical journals and advertisements and in the early Sanitarium brochures.

Strategically built on the elevated terrain of Catholic Hill, on the 100 block of West Main Street, Oakwood stood as a majestic mansion, commanding views of Geneva Lake and the town of Geneva. It had a Main Street frontage spanning a third of a mile with a short walk to the Post Office, and the train station. It encompassed sixty-three acres of scenic beauty adorned with majestic oak trees, lush forests, and gardens traversed by the White River, bordering Lake Elba.

Figure 3: 1891 Plat Map - Mill Pond & Oakwood

Lake Elba was once behind Oakwood Sanitarium. It offered a serene and therapeutic environment for the patients there. Later, it was a popular play area for kids for decades. The pond was drained, and the White River was dredged and re-routed in the 1920s. This was done to make way for Hillmoor's expanding golf course. In the late 1950s, the dam was removed by former Senator William Trinke. The dam's remains were marked by a plaque located at the east end of Haskins Street, on the backside of the 11th hole at Hillmoor's golf course. Although a portion of the stone wall that made up the dam remains, sadly, the historical plaque does not.

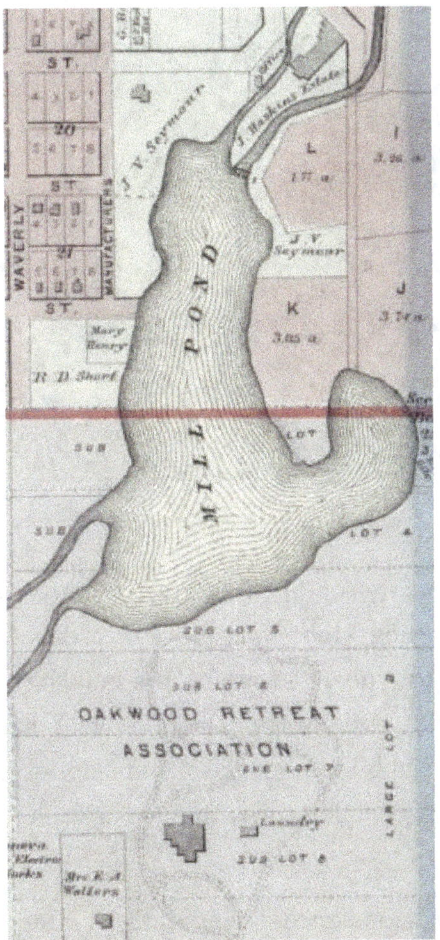

Figure 4: Closer look at 1891 Plat Map - Mill Pond & Oakwood

Offering therapeutic respite with paved ways winding through oaks, meadows, and orchards filled with wildlife. As a model institution, it boasted a construction cost exceeding $100,000.

Figure 5: Oakwood Sanitarium

The original fifty-room, five-story structure was considered fireproof, asserting stone and brick exterior walls featuring hollow spaces for enhanced safety. The building's tall chimneys, spire-like cupolas, and towering red brick walls made it visible for miles. Inside, solid brick inner walls, meticulously plastered from basement to attic, underscored the dedication to durability and security.

The building's opulence extended to its interiors. A majestic marble staircase adorned the main entrance, ushering visitors through floors embellished with mosaic tile and hardwood, thoughtfully separated by a two-inch layer of cement for added resilience. A steel-encased elevator, enveloped by a winding steel stairway adorned with marble steps, transported patients to different floors. The floors were crafted from maple and cherry wood, and the doors were made of butternut.

English Wilton carpets and rugs embellished the floors, while beds boasted the luxury of box springs and hair mattresses. Meticulous planning ensured that each patient enjoyed the comfort of a private room or suite. Some even had private baths, a rarity in those times, which added an extra touch of comfort and dignity. Separate parlors and dining rooms, catering to groups of five to six patients, fostered an atmosphere akin to an elegant hotel or a refined private residence. Dumbwaiters moved between the floors with ease.

Figure 6: Interior of Oakwood Sanitarium; Wisconsin Historical Society, WHI-ID131600:

Oakwood's architectural prowess was complemented by state-of-the-art amenities. Illuminated by the brilliance of electricity and enveloped by the warmth of steam, its ingenious ventilation system could fill a room with smoke and clear it in just ten minutes, eliminating the necessity to open windows or doors. Deafening layers of concrete between floors and carefully constructed walls ensured a serene environment. Thoroughly equipped and furnished, it aspired to offer a haven for healing. The basement contained lesser-discussed details such as iron rings, chains, and isolation cells.

The Sanitarium also contained a separate adjacent laundry building that was connected by an underground tunnel, an icehouse, a woodshop, and other outbuildings.

Figure 7: Oakwood Sanitarium Postcard

On May 13, 1885, Oakwood Sanitarium opened its doors as a private facility catering to the affluent, welcoming a select clientele of the wealthy seeking solace. Designed to accommodate mental and nervous cases requiring guardianship under the leadership of Dr. King, two patients were admitted with three nurses on hand.

The first matron was Kate Wilson, who would continue in that role for six years. She was spoken of quite fondly by H.G. Cutler in the "Medical and Dental Colleges of the West: Historical and Biographical: Chicago," as a lady of rare charms of the heart.

Cutler noted that Kate's "devotion to duty has left a sweet memory of kindness and comfort in the minds of a vast number of once-distracted patients, and her expressions of hope and sympathy brought confidence and cheer to the minds of hundreds of their heartbroken friends."[1]

Then, in August 1887, Dr. Oscar King married Minerva Guernsey, an actress and society lady from Janesville, Wisconsin. Mrs. King planned and conducted indoor and outdoor entertainments for the diversion and amusement of patients—activities such as dances, picnics, educational programs, baseball games, and boat rides.

In 1890, Professor Paul Ziron was a language teacher at the Sanitarium. The Lake Geneva Herald noted that the directors of the Berlitz schools highly recommended him. German and French lessons were given to the patients for therapeutic reasons and to the public.

Oakwood's commitment to excellence was evident in subsequent expansions, with additions in 1889 and 1907 and considerable interior and exterior improvements, demonstrating a dedication to ongoing enhancement.

---

[1] Medical and dental colleges of the West: historical and biographical: Chicago | WorldCat.org. (n.d.). Search.worldcat.org. https://search.worldcat.org/title/7588058

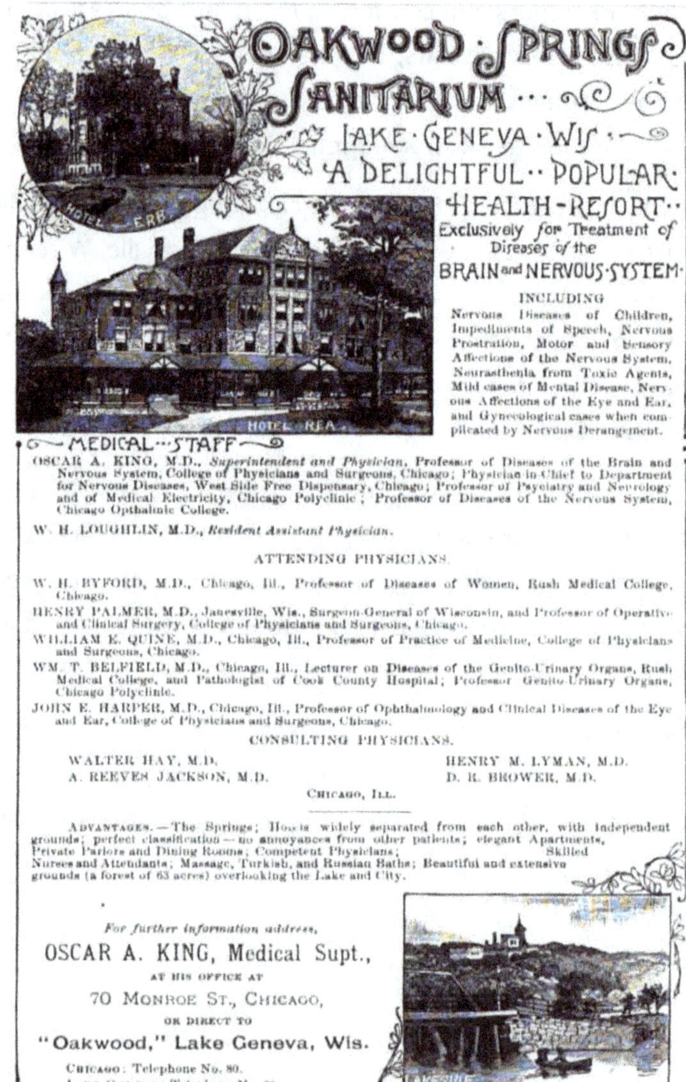

*Figure 8: Advertisement from   The Western Medical Reporter,
Volume 13, Issue 3, 1891*

Figure 9: Oakwood Sanitarium

The financial aspect unfolded as an intricate thread in the tapestry of Oakwood Springs Sanitarium's history.

Section 10, Chapter 171 of the Laws of Wisconsin of 1883, provided an exemption to the Oakwood Retreat Association from assessment and taxation. In 1897, the "Hoyt Bill," repealing the Law of 1883, was ordered to a third reading, claiming that the old law was bad and that it should have never been passed. In 1899, the Lake Geneva Herald announced that a question long in dispute had been settled for good. Bill 88 S. aimed to repeal the section of the law permitting this practice had been approved. The Oakwood Retreat Association was to be fairly and proportionately assessed for taxes, aligning with other property owners' shares.

The cost of respite within its walls amounted to a considerable $500 per month, a costly sum reflected in the exclusive nature of the institution. In addition to this, an extra $40 per month secured the services of a private nurse, ensuring personalized care and attention. Surgical operations, personal laundry, and barber services would incur further costs.

Nutrition played a crucial role in the healthy approach to wellness at Oakwood Sanitarium, which boasted dining halls that served wholesome and nourishing meals prepared by skilled chefs. Dietary counseling was also available to cater to individual needs and preferences. In 1911, the Lake Geneva Herald newspaper reported that Dr. King had completed an "up-to-date dairy" with a good amount of room and electric power that turned on every machine, and he had built the finest refrigerator rooms in Lake Geneva in connection with it.

Within the tranquil halls of Oakwood Springs Sanitarium, a spectrum of treatments unfolded. "Rest Cure" therapy cocooned patients in a sanctuary of quietude and repose, allowing the mind and body to find equilibrium. With its soothing touch, therapeutic massage sought to unravel tension and foster a sense of well-being. The rhythmic embrace of hydrotherapy, echoing through the extensive hydropathical department, offered various treatment baths and exercises.

However, not all approaches were as gentle; "Confinement," a method of its era, was meant to shield patients from external stimuli, allowing the mind to find its balance in solitude. And if the word "hydrotherapy" conjures up images of Hollywood stars lazily soaking in rich, scented baths, then you were **not** a Victorian-era mental patient.

Special treatment rooms were set up that contained large tubs that would be filled with water; if heated, the water would be set between 98°F and 110°F but might reach the scalding temperature of 120°F or more. A thick canvas cover was stretched over the top of the tub and tethered along the rim, with a hole cut out at one end to expose the patient's head.

An attendant would oversee the treatment sessions, during which a patient would be immersed in the tub for hours or, in some cases, days. Warm continuous baths were used to treat patients suffering from insomnia, as well as those considered to be suicidal and assaultive. It was believed that this calmed the excited and agitated behavior. Not surprisingly, these therapies resulted in a state of relaxation or submission, and "Behavioral Compliance" was restored.

Yet another confinement treatment involved mummifying the patient in sheets soaked in ice-cold water. As the sheets dried, they would become tighter around the bound patient. Various hydrotherapeutic techniques involving both hot and cold treatments were used, including Electro-therapeutic hydrotherapy, sprayings from high-pressure showering jets, and alternating scalding to ice baths. This was done with the thought it would shock the insanity out.

Silas Weir Mitchell developed Rest Cure in the late 1800s for the treatment of hysteria and other nervous illnesses, such as Anorexia Nervosa. The usual treatment lasted six to eight weeks. It involved isolation from friends and family. It also enforced bed rest and constant feeding on a fatty, milk-based diet.

Patients were force-fed, if necessary, effectively reducing them to the dependency of an infant. Nurses cleaned and fed the patients and turned them over in their beds. They would also brush their teeth and hair. Doctors used massaging and electrotherapy to maintain muscle tone and avoid atrophy. Patients were sometimes even prohibited from talking, reading, writing, and sewing.

Figure 10: Rest Cure, c. 1890

Mitchell believed the point of the Rest Cure was physical and moral. It boosts the patient's weight and increases blood supply. However, the implicit point was the neurologist breaking his patient's will. Consequently, outspoken, and independent women received the rest cure. These included writers Virginia Woolf and Charlotte Perkins Gilman. They reacted fiercely against the treatment and doctors practicing it, and both wrote about their experiences.

Rest Cure, like hydrotherapy, was a form of "hypnosis" that allowed staff to restrain patients without having to resort to the less palatable alternatives of isolation cells, sedatives, or strait jackets.

In the nineteenth century, neurosyphilis was one of the most ubiquitous and fatal forms of degenerative mental illness known to psychiatry.

"General Paralysis of the Insane" was the term given to a form of neurosyphilis, which is a problem with mental function due to damage to the brain from untreated syphilis. GP patients appeared irritable and forgetful and experienced personality changes, headaches, and changes in sleep habits in the early stage, while emotional lability, impaired memory and judgment, disorientation, confusion, delusions, and occasionally seizures occurred in the late stage.

Amidst the backdrop of these mental health challenges, neurologist Dr. King employed methods, including trepanning, to address neurological disorders. This was the practice of gaining access to the brain by making an incision in the organ's outer casing - in other words, drilling a hole in your head.

Trepanation, an antiquated medical practice involving drilling or cutting holes in the skull, was not only used for treating head injuries but also proved significant in addressing epilepsy and mental illness. It was primarily used for addressing common health issues like migraine headaches and seizures, yet its most renowned application was in treating mental illnesses. This procedure eventually transitioned into the development of the lobotomy, but not before Oakwood would close its doors.

A pharmacopeia of substances could play a vital role in the pursuit of balance. Sedatives such as chloral hydrate, bromides, and barbiturates were carefully administered, orchestrating a delicate dance between tranquility and control. Morphine, cannabis, and even beer found their place in the symphony of remedies tailored to individual needs and sensitivities.

Chloral hydrate was often used to induce sleep and manage anxiety, while bromides and barbiturates provided additional options for calming the nervous system and promoting relaxation.

Morphine, Opium, and Laudanum, potent opioid analgesics, were prescribed to alleviate severe pain. Cannabis-based preparations were utilized at Oakwood Springs Sanitarium for their soothing and anxiolytic properties. These preparations were administered to alleviate symptoms of anxiety, insomnia, and agitation in select patients.

Alcohol, typically in the form of beer, was sometimes prescribed as a sedative or relaxant for patients experiencing heightened anxiety or agitation. Inhaling chloroform was considered a sleep aid. Mercury, known as calomel, was considered an effective treatment for hysteria, but like most of the medicines prescribed for mental illness, it was highly toxic.

Oakwood Sanitarium also recognized the therapeutic benefits of nature for mental and physical rejuvenation. Patients were encouraged to engage in various forms of outdoor recreation, such as hiking, fishing, boating, and horseback riding. The latter proved particularly impactful, offering physical exercise and emotional connection through interaction with these majestic animals. Horses provide comfort, companionship, and confidence-building opportunities for individuals dealing with various psychological challenges or recovering from illnesses.

In addition to outdoor pursuits, Oakwood Sanitarium offered talk therapies, which allowed patients to express their thoughts, feelings, and experiences in a safe environment. These sessions often took place outdoors amidst the serene beauty of the natural surroundings, fostering a sense of calm and introspection. By combining physical activity and psychotherapy, Oakwood Sanitarium created a unique setting where patients could simultaneously address their mental and physical needs.

The emphasis on fresh air was another key component of Oakwood Sanitarium's philosophy. The clean air and spring water were believed to promote better respiratory function and health in general.

According to an article in the Lake Geneva Herald, the large springs at the west end of the park on Lake Elba were analyzed and found to be infused with "the most desirable medicinal qualities, bicarbonate of magnesia being the chief ingredient."[2] Furthermore, exposure to sunlight and vitamin D helped regulate mood and improve immune system functioning.

The names of patients and the resident staff were recorded in the 1900, 1910, and 1920 censuses. (The 1890 census was destroyed in a devastating fire in Washington, D.C.) The roster of Oakwood Sanitarium's patients reads like a who-is-who of the era, with notable figures seeking solace and care within its walls.

The sordid tale of Mrs. Leslie Carter (Caroline Dudley) is a dramatic chapter in the history of Oakwood Sanitarium, weaving together elements of fame, scandal, and mental health. In September 1887, the renowned performer found herself

---

[2] The Lake Geneva Herald Archive. (1916, March 24). Newspapers.com.
https://www.newspapers.com/paper/the-lake-geneva-herald/19689

committed to Oakwood by her husband, setting the stage for a series of events that would capture public attention.

However, Mrs. Carter's stay at Oakwood was short-lived. In November of the same year, she fled the Sanitarium and was accompanied by her visiting young son. This escape, in defiance of Dr. King's assurances to Mr. Carter regarding their son's safety during a visit with Mrs. Carter, marked the beginning of a tumultuous legal and personal journey.

Upon reaching New York, Mrs. Carter promptly filed for divorce, initiating a legal battle that would transfix the public eye. In January 1888, Mr. Carter reciprocated by filing for divorce himself, setting the stage for a protracted and scandalous trial that unfolded through the spring.

Dr. King, intimately involved in Mrs. Carter's case, was called to testify. The 1889 newspaper article from The Inter Ocean sheds light on the medical perspective of Mrs. Carter's condition during her time at Oakwood.

It stated, "After observation of the patient, Dr. King diagnosed mania, which he explained as insanity with exaggeration of emotions with mental excitement and motor derangement. She was sleepless without drugs. Dr. King used every sedative remedy known, once using 80 grains of chloral. He finally used 50 grains of chloral, 25 grains of potassium bromide, and a glass of beer, and after this, the inhalation of chloroform by which treatment she secured about 3 hours of sleep."

Lillian Russell, a renowned actress and the companion of the infamous Diamond Jim Brady found herself among Oakwood's patients.

Ashton Stevens, an influential American journalist, carved out a distinguished career as the dean of American play reviewers and drama critics, with a tenure spanning 50 years, 40 of which were spent with Hearst Newspapers in Chicago. He spent over 18 months on Rest Cure for a severely shattered nervous system.

Mary Gridley Bell, another noteworthy patient, later made a significant contribution to the Lake Geneva community. She stayed at both Oakwood and Lakeside Sanitariums. Her generous donation of $100,000 played a pivotal role in establishing the new Lake Geneva Library. The impact of her philanthropy echoes through the years, leaving an enduring legacy for the benefit of the local community.

Dozens of newspaper articles scattered across the country over the decades form a mosaic of the diverse experiences and challenges faced by Sanitarium patients, both well-known and obscure, providing glimpses into their lives and struggles.

News stories chronicled how patients spiraled, entered Oakwood for treatment, and recovered surprisingly quickly in the case of San Francisco banker John Tallant. On Aug. 26, 1897, The Los Angeles Times and Montana's Anaconda Standard reported that Tallant "Suddenly drew a $20 gold piece from his pocket and threw it with great force at his nearest neighbor. This was followed by a volley of gold coins, which was hurled at the fleeing passengers. Tallant pulled a revolver and flourished it when train hands approached him. Waving his weapon, the man started down the car aisle."

He was bundled off to Oakwood, where after only one day in treatment, the trouble was put down to what the Washington

Times reported on Aug. 27 was "nervous prostration, and that a short rest at Lake Geneva would bring him back to normal condition." It only took one more day before the papers noted, "His mind is now as clear as ever; he is cheerful and in fine physical condition." By Sept. 1, the banker was "entirely recovered from his mental derangement, according to that issue of the Sacramento Bee.

Other patients did not have such speedy recoveries – and then some never had the chance to recover at all. The news coverage of Oakwood included at least three patients over two to three decades who endured challenges beyond the walls of the Sanitarium. Tragic walks along the train tracks, claiming more than one life, cast a shadow on the otherwise serene surroundings of Oakwood Sanitarium and the larger Lake Geneva area.

In addition, reporters caught wind of Habeas Corpus cases such as Charles Edward Shevlin, which was recounted in the St. Louis Post-Dispatch in September of 1903. This "millionaire lumberman of Minneapolis" challenged his diagnosis and confinement via the courts. Circumstances such as Shevlin's, along with the inevitable presence of suicides, underscored the legal and emotional challenges embedded in the discipline of mental health care in a time when institutionalization was often the recourse for those deemed "too insane." (The move to Wisconsin Hospital for the Insane, which later became known as Mendota State Hospital, was for patients whose needs exceeded Oakwood's aptitude.)

Newspaper articles from the era also captured the multifaceted nature of life within and around the Sanitarium as the lives of patients intersected with the broader community. Wandering patients, a collective worry among the townsfolk, served as a recurring motif throughout the stories. The town became a community where the residents grappled with the nuances of coexisting with a Sanitarium.

In 1893, the exasperated foreman for Geo L Dunlap wrote an editorial complaining about patients "...using language not fit for a man to hear, to say nothing of the ladies who were walking on the lake shore." [3]

But while the patients' unauthorized excursions were an irritant, the more pressing concern was the safety of both locals and patients. Then 'The Lake Geneva Herald' claimed that an Oakwood resident, Judge Stitt, "wandered down to the lakeshore. When he arrived at C.M. Baker's pier, he took off his hat, laid down his cane, and jumped in deliberately. He immediately tried to rescue himself but would have failed had it not been for Mr. C.M. Baker, who assisted him. These patients should always be accompanied by an attendant." [4]

The veil of anonymity shrouding patients, checking in under false names, adds a layer of mystery to the narratives. The spectrum of patient experiences unfolds in the tales of those who went missing, later found accidentally drowned, or those who had merely returned home. The dichotomy of relief and grief

---

[3] Humanities, N. E. for the. (n.d.). The Lake Geneva herald. [volume]. Chroniclingamerica.loc.gov. Retrieved April 30, 2024, from https://chroniclingamerica.loc.gov/lccn/sn85040075/

[4] Oakwood. (1905, December 29). The Lake Geneva Herald, 1. https://www.newspapers.com/article/the-lake-geneva-herald-oakwood/58869759/

intertwined in these stories reflects the complexities of mental health care during the historical period.

These stories, each a chapter in the collective history of the sanitarium, transcend the pages of newspapers, reaching across time to shed light on the intricacies of mental health care, societal perceptions, and the shared journey of those who walked the corridors of the institution…

The year 1921 marked a pivotal moment in the history of Oakwood and the Lake Geneva Sanitariums with the passing of Dr. King, who died of arthritis and exhaustion.

Following his demise, his wife, Minerva, and the staff undertook the responsibility of managing the sanitariums. Their efforts persisted until 1927, but unfortunately, financial difficulties forced the closure of Oakwood.

Dr. George A. Post was Dr. King's assistant physician at the sanitariums from 1899 to 1901, when he moved to Chicago, Illinois, and went into general practice. In 1921, he returned to being medical superintendent.

After Dr. King's death, Dr. Post played a pivotal role in advocating the Oakwood property to the United States Veteran's Bureau, envisioning its purchase and conversion into a VA hospital dedicated to aiding disabled soldiers afflicted with shell shock and other mental disorders. Sadly, this would never be.

On May 3, 1926, Judge Roscoe Luce ordered a judgment of foreclosure. It was decided that the sanitariums could be operated for one year under the receivership of Henry D.L. Atkins, vice president of the First National Bank of Elkhorn. The judgment added, "If at the end of that time, the bonds have not been redeemed, the property will be sold, including the Cottage, to satisfy the first mortgage."[5]

In June 1927, the State of Wisconsin, Walworth County, held a Notice of Foreclosure Sale. Nathan Shure, a wealthy Chicago manufacturer, purchased the building and grounds for $55,000 in back taxes. He acquired the corporation's stock and began to sell but kept the Oakwood building and the immediate grounds and allowed continued use under the new management.

On May 15, 1928, the dissolution of the articles of organization of the Lake Geneva Sanitariums was filed with the register of deeds. Oakwood Sanitarium closed, and patients moved to Lakeside Sanitarium.

The 1930 Census of Lake Geneva still lists patients & staff under "The Lake Geneva Sanitariums." However, an article in the Lake Geneva Regional News on December 18, 1930, states that "Oakwood Sanitarium had been moved the past week to its new location on the south shore of the lake, having recently purchased the J.L. Guyon property which is next to the Lake Geneva Club. According to Dr. J.D. Warrick, superintendent, the institution's name has been changed to the Lake Geneva Health Resort."

Unfortunately, the fate of the building took a somber turn as it stood vacant for over four decades. The echoes of Oakwood Sanitarium lingered in the silence that engulfed the vacant structure as it was vandalized and frequented by transients and local youth.

---

[5] The Lake Geneva Regional News Archive. (2001, March 1). Newspapers.com. https://www.newspapers.com/paper/the-lake-geneva-regional-news/19685/

Figure 11: Oakwood Sanitarium photo from Dr. Robert White

In 1947, Hobart Hermanson paid $45,000 for the building and grounds. The once-stately Sanitarium faced the destructive forces of multiple fires in the 1950s, leaving it in a state of disrepair and ruin.

The first significant fire was in 1950, and the article "Geneva May Condemn Old Oakwood Retreat" appeared in the Janesville Daily Gazette on November 4, 1950. In November 1953 and then October 1956, two more major fires ravaged Oakwood. The last fire in 1956 left the building in ruins. Owner avoidance and weather delays filled the years 1957 and 1958. Finally, in 1959, Oakwood was demolished. The foundation ruins remained until the late 1970s, when the Havenwood construction began.

Figure 12: Oakwood Sanitarium photo from Vince Danca

While necessary for safety reasons and urban development, the process of razing the building symbolized the end of a significant chapter in the history of Lake Geneva and mental health treatment.

Chapter 3: Lakeside Sanitarium (1893 – 1930) and Lakeside Cottage (1896 – 1926)

The sanitariums stood as monuments to the King Family, with Dr. King's brothers, Riley G., and Albert E. King, making significant financial contributions to acquire Lakeside Sanitarium and Lakeside Cottage. Riley and his wife resided with the doctor at Oakwood Sanitarium until their return to Indiana in 1900. Their continued visits during the Sanitarium's operation underscored the enduring family connection.

Figure 13: Lakeside Sanitarium Advertisement

In the transformative year of 1893, Lakeside Sanitarium emerged as a new chapter in the story. It was acquired and attentively designed under discerning guidance for treating medical and general sanitarium cases. Nestled half a mile from its sister institution, Oakwood, Lakeside offers a rich history.

Originally, the building served as the dormitory for the Lake Geneva Seminary, a ladies' school with its structure dating back to the 1860s. It was a three-story brick building with floor-to-ceiling windows on the first two floors and a palatial facade. The largest dining room was often used for dances and social activities.

Figure 14: Lake Geneva Seminary campus.

Figure 15: Lakeside Sanitarium

It was purchased from the Charles Minton Baker family for medical purposes, distinguishing it from the upscale Oakwood Sanitarium. Situated ideally on the shores of Lake Geneva, it offered breathtaking views and easy access to the lake's calming waters. Lakeside Sanitarium catered to patients needing various general medical treatments. Doctors from Chicago were welcomed to bring their patients and nurses to the facilities for treatment.

In 1896, a modern system of baths – electric, thermal, and others - was added to the Sanitarium.

1896 was the same year that Lakeside Sanitarium expanded its embrace when the building next door was acquired for use and renamed "Lakeside Cottage." It was constructed in 1885 as a summer retreat for Mrs. Robert Hall Baker (Emily) as a loving tribute to her late husband. The land that the house was built on was initially given to C.M. Baker (Robert's father) in 1838 by the city of Lake Geneva as part of a "compensation package" for becoming the first District Attorney of Walworth County.

Figure 16: Lakeside Sanitarium postcard

The Queen Anne Mansion was initially christened "Redwood Cottage," with the exterior shingles exclusively crafted from majestic Californian Redwoods. Intricately carved into thousands of original shingles were seven distinct ornate patterns, displaying craftsmanship paralleled only by the pristine stained glass and hand-planed custom doors. There were thirteen grand fireplaces surrounded by floor-to-ceiling hand-carved mantles embellished with pristine J & JG Low Art Tile of Chelsea, Massachusetts. The ornate inlaid wood floors were made from five species of wood adorning the residence.

Figure 17: Lakeside Cottage Sanitarium postcard

Mrs. Baker continued to use the summer home until she died in 1894. After her death, the property passed to Robert Baker, Jr., who sold the house to Celinda Walkup. Mrs. Walkup continued to operate the cottage as an annex to Lakeside Sanitarium until she died in 1905. Her daughter, Luella Johnston, would eventually sell the cottage and property to Dr. King in 1910.

A new operating room was completed in 1918 at Lakeside, which added a new electrical apparatus that equipped the facility for X-ray diagnosis and radiology. A brochure indicates that the thoroughly equipped laboratories contained instruments of accuracy and methods of precision and that the X-ray, chemical, and biological laboratories were in constant service.

The Lakeside Sanitarium campus included two buildings and ten acres of land. The lake gracefully bordered the grounds to the front and west, while Seminary/Maxwell Park enclosed the eastern edge. Expansive porches, sunlit lawns, majestic trees, and ample shade complemented the offerings of Geneva Lake.

Figure 18: Lakeside Sanitarium postcard

In the "History of Walworth County Wisconsin," Albert Beckwith stated, "One entering Lakeside or the Cottage sees nothing to suggest a habitation for the sick. The halls and parlors are well furnished, fresh, and bright and suggest a private home rather than an institution."

This period saw the emergence of new ideas about the care and treatment of mental illness, including the development of moral treatment, which promised a cure for mental illnesses to those who sought treatment in a new kind of hospital that provided quiet, secluded, and peaceful country settings, opportunities for meaningful work and recreation, a system of privileges and rewards for rational behaviors, and gentler kinds of restraints used for shorter periods.

Able patients were treated to a myriad of recreational opportunities, including boating, fishing, sailing, croquet, tennis, horseback riding, and driving during the summer months, either alone or accompanied by their attendants.

The landscape transformed into a playground for sleighing, skating, ice-boat sailing, and other invigorating winter sports in winter. The facilities themselves provided indoor diversions such as billiards, books, music, dancing, and social entertainment, ensuring that every season brought a spectrum of activities for the well-being and enjoyment of the residents.

The cottage addition marked a strategic enhancement to the Lakeside Sanitarium campus, broadening its capabilities and offerings in medical care. Lakeside Cottage would be used for "Light Nervous Disorders," melancholia, and recovering addicts.

Sadly, only a few generations ago, women who suffered from work stress, post-partum depression, anorexia nervosa, anxiety attacks, or even exhaustion were often confined to an asylum. Incorrigible and strong-willed women were also committed, along with addicts and the insane.

In the late 1800s and early 1900s, mental illnesses started receiving names such as 'Melancholia' (known as 'Depression' today), 'Schizophrenia,' and 'Circular Insanity' (which today is known as Bipolar and was previously Manic Depressive).

Lakeside Cottage was closed and sold in 1926. Lakeside Sanitarium would continue to operate until 1928 under the management of Mrs. King and the dedicated staff.

Figure 19: Lakeside Cottage Stone Pillar

Figure 20: Lakeside & Cottage Stone Pillars

The evolution of the property unearthed relics of its past. In 1983, an excavation crew collaborated with the owners during the renovation of the St. Moritz. They uncovered the original columns that once lined the driveway entrance to the Lakeside and Lakeside Cottage Sanitariums. Standing as a silent witness to bygone eras, these architectural remnants surfaced from the earth to share their stories, only to be returned to the ground.

Chapter 4: The Surgery (1906 – 1925)

The cryptic sentence, *"Sometime later, Mr. Walter's home would become the surgery,"* proved to be a challenging clue. This single sentence was all that Albert C. Beckwith had to offer on the topic in "The History of Walworth County." Unraveling this mystery led to fascinating discoveries of the historical evolution of Oakwood Sanitarium. Tantalizing clues emerged from the depth of time, offering glimpses into its purpose and significance.

As my research progressed, it became clear that the cottage belonging to Mr. J.C. Walter found a new purpose within the grounds of Oakwood. Dr. King's mother-in-law arrived, leasing the Walter cottage in 1890. This private residence became integrated into the fabric of Oakwood Sanitarium.

Figure 21: The Surgery

The structure was hidden away. It was tucked into an expansive lawn and shaded by a grove of large oak trees, and the cottage boasted a spacious veranda stretching from the front to the side of the building, away from the Sanitarium. Floor-to-ceiling windows on both floors gave way to abundant natural light and fresh air perfectly suited for healing. Sharing the same 63-acre property, patients could convalesce in the beauty of natural surroundings. Despite its mysterious presence, historical research reveals that the surgery was far from a mere enigma; it stood as a testament to the progressive ethos of its time.

Figure 22: The Surgery Lawn

Fast forward to 1906, and Lake Geneva stood on the cusp of a significant milestone. The Lake Geneva Regional News heralded the establishment of an Operating Hospital within the town. Characterized by its advanced equipment, rigorous cleanliness standards, and state-of-the-art operating room, this hospital aimed to deliver top-notch medical services to the local community.

It was readily apparent that Dr. King possessed a strong inclination towards continually seeking out and incorporating the most recent advancements and innovative technology into the sanitarium facilities. Alongside his intense interest in medicine and psychiatry, King also dedicated himself to technological endeavors, as evidenced by his involvement in two patent applications from 1893 in collaboration with Dr. Post.

An advertisement from the era provides insight into the unique characteristics of the surgery: a distinct building devoted solely to surgical cases. It highlighted state-of-the-art features, such as a meticulously crafted operating room equipped with the latest antiseptic measures—a clear symbol of modernity and hygiene within the medical profession.

Figure 23: An advertisement for Lake Geneva Sanitariums

Within its walls, spacious bedrooms bathed in natural light welcomed patients, offering respite and comfort in times of ailment. Accompanying these quarters were well-appointed baths, ensuring the maintenance of cleanliness and sanitation—a crucial aspect of medical care. Equally important, a dedicated diet kitchen stood ready to cater to the dietary needs of recovering patients.

Regrettably, historical records remain silent, leaving a void in the narrative of Oakwood's evolution of the Surgery. Yet, its legacy endures—a symbol of progress, compassion, and innovation in the annals of medical history.

As Oakwood stood vacant, the surgery was inhabited by Hobart Hermansen's workers. Hobart and his brother Einar were the sons of Christian Hermansen, who purchased the Como Hotel in 1921 and bought the Lake Geneva Hotel in the 1930s. Hobart was a known friend to Chicago Prohibition-era gangster Bugs Moran. In 1958, the Lake Geneva Regional News reported that a "Man Cut with Knife During Friendly Scuffle" had taken place in the tenant house of Oakwood Sanitarium.

Continuing to obscure Oakwood's mysterious past and its accompanying structures, the surgery served as evidence of the enduring spirit of advancement and care that defined an era. Its story, though fragmented, serves as a poignant reminder of the indelible mark left by those who dared to push the boundaries of convention and embrace the relentless pursuit of excellence.

Chapter 5: The Lake Geneva Sanitariums (1901 – 1928)

The consolidation of Oakwood Springs Sanitarium and the Lakeside Sanitarium campus in 1901 marked a significant turning point. This merger resulted in the formation of the "Lake Geneva Sanitariums," representing a unified entity dedicated to providing comprehensive medical care.

By bringing together multiple institutions under a single name, the Lake Geneva Sanitariums aimed to leverage both entities' combined resources, expertise, and facilities. This consolidation led to several benefits:

Streamlined Operations: Combining the administrative, medical, and operational functions of two separate institutions streamlined processes and reduced redundancies. This could have resulted in more efficient use of resources and improved coordination among staff members.

Enhanced Efficacy: With shared facilities and personnel, the Lake Geneva Sanitariums could optimize their operations to better meet their patients' needs. This may have included improved scheduling, standardized treatment protocols, and better medical equipment and supplies utilization.

Strengthened Reputation: The consolidation of Oakwood Springs and Lakeside Sanitariums under a single name enhanced the institution's reputation within the community and beyond. A unified brand conveyed a sense of stability, expertise, and commitment to quality care, attracting patients from a wider geographical area.

Expanded Services: By combining their resources, the Lake Geneva Sanitariums may have expanded the range of medical services offered to patients. This could include access to specialized treatments, new medical technologies, and a broader network of healthcare professionals

The seventy-three acres of picturesque woodlands surrounding the separate institutions played a crucial role in shaping the reputation of the sanitariums and solidifying Dr. King's status as a pioneer in the medical field. The doctor's creative approach focused on creating an environment conducive to healing by placing nervous patients in serene and aesthetically pleasing surroundings.

By situating the sanitariums amidst beautiful woodlands, Dr. King aimed to shield patients from the stresses and disturbances of everyday life, providing them with a tranquil retreat where they could focus on their recovery. This thoughtful approach demonstrated his compassion for his patients and reflected his understanding of the therapeutic benefits of natural surroundings on mental health and well-being.

Patients of the sanitariums received attentive care and close monitoring from experienced physicians and nurses, further emphasizing Dr. King's commitment to providing optimal conditions for healing and recovery. The combination of serene surroundings, expert medical care, and personalized attention contributed to the reputation of the sanitariums as leading institutions for treating nervous disorders.

Dr. King's visionary approach to patient care set the standard for modern healthcare practices. His forward-thinking methods benefited patients at the time and laid the groundwork for advancements in holistic and patient-centered care in the years to come.

The two-page color-headed spread in the Lake Geneva Regional News in 1909 showcased the significance of the Lake Geneva Sanitariums to the local community. The header of the coverage, titled "The Importance of the Institutions to Lake Geneva," promised readers a comprehensive account of the founding and development of the sanitariums, along with a biographical sketch of the founder and insights into the future direction of the institutions.

The piece provided readers with valuable insights into the historical background of the sanitariums, highlighting their role in shaping the local economy. Overall, the coverage in the Lake Geneva Regional News served as a tribute to the importance of the Lake Geneva Sanitariums to the local community, highlighting their historical significance, contributions to healthcare, and vision for the future. It fostered a sense of pride and appreciation among readers for the institutions that played such a vital role in the life of Lake Geneva.

Figure 24: Lake Geneva Regional News 1909 - Page 1

Figure 25: Lake Geneva Regional News 1909 - Page 2

Within a decade of this transition, the Lake Geneva Sanitariums took another monumental step forward: In January 1910, a training school for nurses was opened. This initiative demonstrated a commitment to providing exceptional medical care and nurturing the next generation of healthcare professionals.

The course period of three years included the following curriculum: Anatomy, Physiology, Toxicology, Practical Chemistry, Psychology, Sense Training (*a group of techniques designed to improve the functioning of different sensory systems and perceptions*), and Domestic Sciences such as cooking and dietetics. Other subjects covered were Obstetrics, Disease, Injury, Habits, Preparation of patients for examinations, and operating room. As well as Asepsis (*the practice of keeping an area free of germs to prevent infection*) and Dressings. In addition, the future nurses received instruction and practiced in baths, hydrotherapy, Electricity, Massage, and Swedish Movements.

Figure 26: Lake Geneva Training School for Nurses

In 1910, when the staff were asked to fill out a census form during the Census of Oakwood Sanitariums, they shared no other information than the name and gender of the current patients. The census taker noted, **"Physician refused to answer, and people were too insane."**

The sanitariums served as a major source of income for the community, providing employment opportunities for locals and generating substantial revenue from patients.

From 1885 to 1925, the sanitariums maintained steady growth, with annual earnings ranging from $85,000 to $100,000. This consistent income played a crucial role in supporting the local economy.

In 1924, the Lake Geneva Regional News reported that "The bookkeeping department of the sanitariums has been conducted by a system of monthly and annual reports of earnings and expenses. In examining these reports, we find that the actual money expended in maintaining the running businesses from 1885 to 1925 - 40 years – about $3,000,000, and the great bulk of this money has been paid to the merchants of Lake Geneva for building and living supplies."[6]

The reliance on local merchants for supplies underscores the symbiotic relationship between the sanitariums and the community. The economic success of the sanitariums contributed significantly to the prosperity of Lake Geneva.

---

[6] Lake Geneva News Tribune (Lake Geneva, Wis.) 1924-1933. (n.d.). Library of Congress, Washington, D.C. 20540 USA. Retrieved May 8, 2024, from https://www.loc.gov/item/sn87082110/

Timeline of the "Lake Geneva Sanitariums" Campus

1883 – The "Oakwood Retreat Association" is founded by Dr. Oscar A. King & Dr. Henry Palmer of Janesville.

1884 – Construction is started on Oakwood.

1885 – May 13th, Oakwood Retreat is opened as a private sanitarium or insane asylum for the wealthy. Intended for mental and nervous cases requiring guardianship.

1887 – August 9th, Dr. Oscar King marries Minerva Guernsey.

1889 – Addition built onto Oakwood.

1890 – Mrs. Sarah Guernsey (mother to Minerva & Sara) leases J.C. Walter's cottage.

1891 – July 22nd, Dr. George Post marries Sara Guernsey.

1892 – June 23rd, Helen Minerva Post is born at Oakwood.

1893 - Lakeside Sanitarium would be acquired and opened for medical/general cases.

1896 - Lakeside Cottage is acquired.

1901 – Oakwood, Lakeside Sanitarium & Lakeside Cottage are incorporated as the "Lake Geneva Sanitariums."

1906 – The Surgery is established.

1907 – 2nd Addition built onto Oakwood.

1909 – November 19th, 1909, public notice is given in Lake Geneva Regional News that Oakwood Retreat Association has legally changed its name to the Lake Geneva Sanitariums.

1909 – December 16th, Lake Geneva Regional News runs 2-page color-headed coverage.

1910 – A training school for Nurses is opened.

1921 – September 11th, Dr. Oscar A. King dies at Oakwood, Dr. Post is the attending physician.

1926 – Foreclosure of Oakwood and Lakeside Cottage; Bought by Nathan Shure for back taxes.

1928 – May 15th, The Dissolution of the Articles of Organization of the Lake Geneva Sanitariums is filed with the register of deeds. Oakwood Sanitarium is closed, and its patients are moved to Lakeside. The building was vacant until razed.

1930 – Remaining Lakeside patients moved to J.L. Guyon property on the south shore (next to Lake Geneva Club) The name was changed to Lake Geneva Health Resort.

1947 - Owned by Einar and Hobart Hermanson.

1950s – Ravaged by several fires. It was vandalized and frequented by transients and local youth.

1959 – Oakwood Sanitarium is razed.

1970 – Hotel Luzerne, formerly Lakeside Sanitarium, is razed & the basement ruins of Oakwood are removed for the construction of Havenwood Apartments & Colonial Condominiums.

Chapter 6: Oscar August King, M. D.

Figure 27: Oscar August King

In the narrative of the Sanitariums of Lake Geneva, a few remarkable individuals illuminate the story with their extraordinary lives. Among them is Oscar Augustus King. Born on February 22, 1851, in Peru, Indiana, his journey is a captivating tale of academic brilliance, unwavering dedication to medicine, and groundbreaking strides in neurology and psychiatry.

As we begin this chapter, we immerse ourselves in the impressive life of Oscar Augustus King—replete with perseverance, passion, and notable contributions to the betterment of humanity.

Born to Timothy Lewis King and Mary Maria Wright, Oscar was the seventh of eleven children in the family. Growing up on his father's farm, King showed early promise in school. He graduated as valedictorian from Peru High School. After that, he spent years teaching before deciding to become a doctor.

King began his medical studies in 1873 under the guidance of Professor Henry Palmer of Janesville, Wisconsin, and the Surgeon-General of Wisconsin. The journey led him to Belleville

Hospital Medical College, New York, where he was a private student of Professor Louis A. Sayre of New York and graduated in 1878. Subsequently, he joined the Wisconsin State Hospital for the Insane at Madison as Second Assistant Physician.

After the board of trustees granted him a leave of absence in 1880, Dr. King began a transformative journey to the University of Vienna, Austria, studying the clinics of Moritz Kaposi and Theodor Billroth. He delved deep into neurology and psychiatry there under renowned professors Maximilian Leidesdorf, Deso Weiss, Moritz Benedikt, and Theodor Meynert. This experience enriched his knowledge and laid the foundation for his future contributions.

Upon returning home, Dr. King resumed his medical career. He advanced to the position of First Assistant Physician at the Wisconsin State Hospital for the Insane. In 1882, he took on the role of teaching Mental and Nervous Diseases at the College of Physicians and Surgeons in Chicago.

Over time, he garnered recognition and additional responsibilities within the institution, eventually becoming a director and serving as Secretary. By 1896, his teaching title had evolved to Professor of Neurology, Psychiatry, and Clinical Medicine.

In addition to his academic endeavors, Dr. King's influence extended to healthcare institutions. He initiated his efforts methodically, starting by advocating for the passage of appropriate laws governing such institutions in the 1883 legislature. Dr. King's proposed bills were successfully passed with only a minor amendment. These statutes played a pivotal role in inspiring the establishment of numerous sanitariums across the state of Wisconsin.

In 1884, he founded Oakwood Springs Sanitarium in Lake Geneva, Wisconsin, a significant milestone in his dedication to treating nervous and mental diseases.

Dr. King's personal life played a significant role in shaping his legacy. His marriage in 1887 to Miss Minerva Guernsey from Janesville, Wisconsin, was a pivotal moment. She graduated from the Frances Willard School and Boston University, class of 1879. She had a successful career as an actress and interpreter of literature with the Booth and Barrett acting company.

Mrs. King, distinguished by her cultivated and refined tastes, brought a unique perspective to their partnership. While not particularly drawn to medical topics, she exhibited a keen interest in general sciences, a deep devotion to literature, and a remarkable ability to critique art.

She took on the responsibility of organizing and conducting educational and entertainment activities to keep the patients at Oakwood Springs Sanitarium engaged and entertained. Her dedication did not go unnoticed, earning her the respect and admiration of patients and loyal nurses.

The union of Oscar King and Minerva Guernsey exemplified a harmonious blend of intellectual pursuits and shared values. Together, they contributed to Lake Geneva's cultural and scientific landscape, leaving a legacy through the institutions founded by Dr. King for the compassionate and progressive care of those facing mental health challenges.

In 1890, Mrs. Sarah Guernsey, mother to Minerva, leased J.C. Walter's cottage. This transaction marked a chapter in the cottage's narrative and hinted at the intriguing tales and connections that unfolded within its walls during that era.

Figure 28: Informal Group at Oakwood Sanitarium; Wisconsin Historical Society, WHI-ID115959

The story then progresses to 1891, with the noteworthy marriage between Dr. George A. Post and Sarah May Guernsey on July 21st. This union not only joined two individuals but also forged familial ties that would significantly influence the trajectory of Oakwood.

Following this pivotal event, on June 23rd, 1892, Helen Minerva Post, the niece of Dr. King, was born at Oakwood. She further strengthened the family bonds within the Sanitarium's community, later accompanying her aunt Minerva traveling and becoming involved in the operations at Oakwood.

—Dr. and Mrs. George A. Post, of "Oakwood" are rejoicing at the arrival of a big bright baby at their new home last week Thursday morning.

Figure 29: Helen Post is Born - LG Herald 7.1.1892

It is also important to note that Dr. King's influence extended far beyond his role as a physician. In 1900, he played a crucial part as the committee chair head on university relations, significantly contributing to the integration of the College of Physicians and Surgeons into the University of Illinois. His dedication to various institutions, such as the Illinois College of Dentistry, illustrated his commitment to advancing medical education and practice.

In 1901, Dr. King continued demonstrating his vision and leadership by consolidating the campuses of Oakwood Springs Sanitarium, The Surgery, Lakeside Sanitarium, and Lakeside Cottage to establish the "Lake Geneva Sanitariums." This initiative marked a significant milestone in providing mental health care in the Lake Geneva area, highlighting Dr. King's ongoing dedication to improving healthcare infrastructure and accessibility.

However, the winter of 1918 brought an unexpected and challenging turn for Dr. King. On the last day of February, he slipped on ice, resulting in a severe injury to his ankle. Unfortunately, what initially seemed like a straightforward incident turned into a more complicated health issue. Dr. King developed internal complications, including a severe mixed infection affecting his nose, throat, and bronchial tubes. This condition led to a severe toxemic state, forcing him to remain confined to his bed for several weeks.

Throughout this period, the physicians overseeing Dr. King's care deemed his condition dangerously ill. The internal complications, combined with the aftermath of the ankle injury, presented a significant health challenge for the founder and president of the Lake Geneva Sanitariums. His absence from his usual activities undoubtedly left a noticeable void within the community.

By May, there emerged a glimmer of hope when Dr. U.G. Darling, superintendent of the Lake Geneva Sanitariums, announced that Dr. King was on the road to recovery. The attending physicians expressed optimism that he would soon resume his active role in managing the sanitariums, suggesting a return to his usual vigor. The community would have eagerly awaited Dr. King's full recovery, recognizing the importance of his leadership in the realm of mental and nervous health care.

However, due to Dr. King's severe illness in 1921, Dr. Post returned to the sanitariums as medical superintendent. On September 11, 1921, Dr. Oscar King's passing marked a heartbreaking moment in the history of Oakwood and the Lake Geneva Sanitariums.

The funeral services held at the United Congregational Church garnered a remarkable turnout, indicative of the widespread respect and fondness for the departed doctor. Reverend Wilson Denney, pastor of the church, presided over the solemn occasion. The presence of a large congregation underscored the significant impact the departed had on the community, as friends, family, colleagues, and acquaintances came together to honor and celebrate his memory. After the services, Dr. King's body was taken to Janesville, Wisconsin, to be met by a group of Janesville physicians and citizens. Burial followed in Oak Hill Cemetery there.

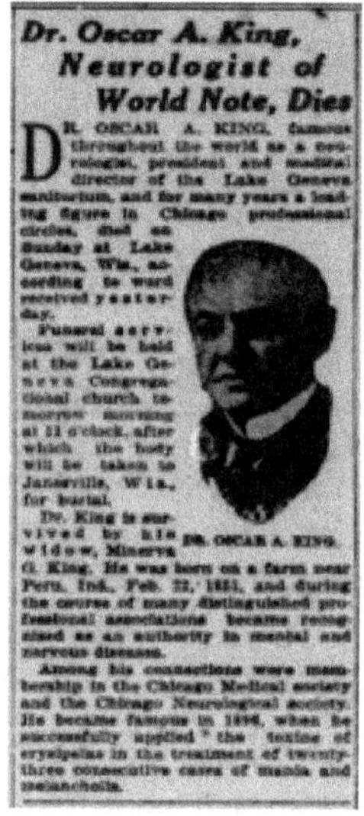

Figure 30: News About Dr. Oscar August King's Death

At the time of his passing, Dr. King held the esteemed title of Professor of Neurology and Psychiatry Emeritus at the University's College of Medicine, a role he dutifully fulfilled without ever missing a lecture. Despite the distance, he regularly commuted between Lake Geneva and Chicago, often taking the red-eye train. Dr. King was actively involved in various medical organizations, including the University Club of Chicago, the Advisory Medical Board at the Cook County institutions at Dunning, the Chicago Medical Society, the Wisconsin State Medical Society, and the American Medical Association.

His death certificate attributes arthritis and exhaustion as the cause of his demise, with Dr. George A. Post, his brother-in-law, signing it.

The kinship between Dr. King and Dr. Post, who were both married to the Guernsey sisters, enhanced the sense of community and shared responsibility within Oakwood's leadership. The meaningful connection among these key figures enriches Oakwood's intricate history, intertwining personal and professional relationships within the world of healthcare provision and administration.

Following Dr. King's passing, his wife, her sister, brother-in-law, and the devoted staff managed the sanitariums, a duty they conducted until 1928. However, the period after 1921 contained challenges for the institutions, particularly financial constraints, significantly impacting their ongoing operation. The closure of Oakwood and the dissolution of the sanitariums symbolize the conclusion of an era, signifying a shift in the historical trajectory of these healthcare facilities.

Dr. King's enduring legacy is prominently evident in his pivotal role as the founder and Chief of Staff of the Lake Geneva Sanitariums, where he dedicated an impressive 37 years of his career. His leadership, diverse skill set, and unwavering dedication played a vital role in establishing one of the country's most comprehensive and renowned private sanitariums, leaving a lasting mark on the field of mental health care.

Chapter 7: Notables, Local Lore, and The End

Special places hold a treasure trove of stories, and the Lake Geneva Sanitariums are no exception. From famous visitors leaving their mark to tales whispered through generations, these sanitariums have a rich tapestry of memories and mysteries waiting to be explored. Let us delve into the fascinating anecdotes and legends that have shaped the history of these iconic institutions.

Anecdotes and Legends:

In 1887, the Lake Geneva Fresh Air Association was founded, paving the way for establishing the Holiday Home Camp. This initiative aimed to provide enriching experiences for older children, including visits to Oakwood Sanitarium, fostering educational growth alongside outdoor activities. Some of the Chicago ladies and club officers included Mrs. Simeon B. Chapin, Miss Alma Seipp, Mrs. C. Seipp, and Mrs. R. T. Crane.

The "McDonald's Medical Directory" of 1889 offers a glimpse into the advertising landscape of the era, with eight pages dedicated to promoting the Sanitariums. These advertisements, accompanied by captivating sketches by John Bullock, provide insight into the promotional strategies of the time, highlighting the allure of these healthcare facilities.

Similarly, the 1895 "Connorton's (formerly McDonald's) Medical Directory" serves as a testament to the ongoing popularity of Oakwood Springs and Bayhouse Sanitariums

(Lakeside). Featuring these establishments on its cover, along with informative advertisements and additional sketches by John Bullock, the directory offers a comprehensive overview of the services and amenities available at these renowned sanitariums.

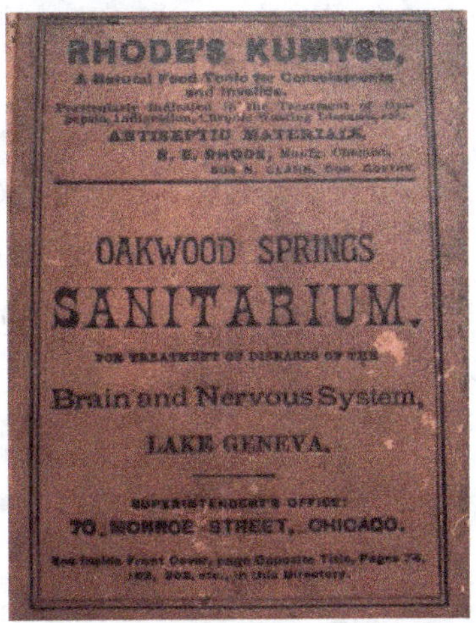

Figure 31: Rhode's Medical Directory

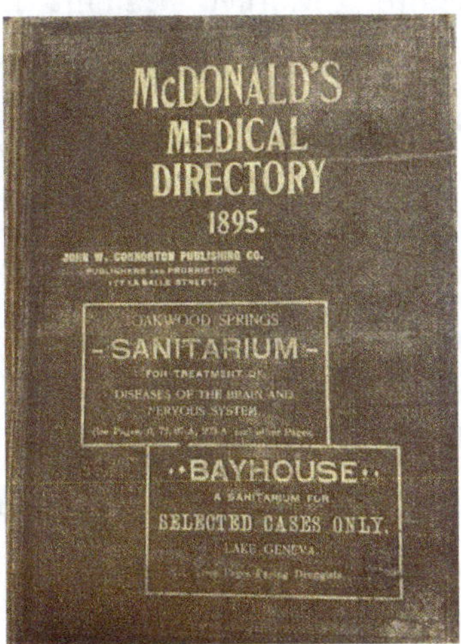

Figure 32: McDonald's Medical Directory

The Geneva Lake Museum hosts an intriguing piece of history: an authentic 1897 stock certificate acquired by Sydney Kuh, a notable Chicago physician and psychiatrist. Kuh's professional endeavors extended to the Chicago House of Correction, where he dedicated himself to treating patients within the criminal justice system. His practice delved into complex debates surrounding insanity, mental illness, and their connection to criminal behavior. As a sympathetic physician, Kuh advocated for viewing prisoners with mental disorders as individuals in need of medical care rather than as mere criminals deserving punishment.

Among the events and objects of the early 1900s, figures emerged whose contributions left a lasting impact on their communities.

Around 1918, Clara Richter Heiden began her employment at Oakwood Sanitarium, taking on the role of laundress. However, as her granddaughter, Marilyn Heiden recounted, Clara's responsibilities often stretched beyond laundry duties. She occasionally found herself in the kitchen, cooking meals, particularly when the designated cook could not fulfill his duties due to intoxication. During these times, Clara would step in to prepare meals, and her young daughter would assist in managing the laundry alongside her.

This transition from daily tasks to multifaceted roles highlights the resilience of individuals like Clara and the importance of their contributions within institutions like Oakwood Sanitarium. These dedicated individuals worked behind the scenes to ensure the sanitarium operated smoothly during challenging circumstances.

Resident Donald Henry told the story of being a child who used to fish in Lake Elba. He would take his catch to Oakwood and sell it to the residents, who were then referred to as "inmates."

Another recollection comes from Vern Hackett, a local businessman, who used to deliver newspapers to Oakwood every evening, "and often heard screams – and nearly always heard a pianist of concert caliber."

Macabre myths and gossip existed and still make the rounds today, but like other such outlandish local legends, have never been substantiated.

A scandal rocked the City of Lake Geneva around 1922, revolving around Josiah Barfield, who served as the treasurer of Oakwood Retreat Association and then the Lake Geneva Sanitariums between 1890 and 1922. Barfield held various other prestigious positions in the community, including treasurer roles at the Lake Geneva Country Club, Lake Geneva Library, Lake Geneva Episcopal Church, and as a trusted cashier at the First National Bank. However, in 1922, he faced arrest for embezzling $14,000 from his cousin.

Exploiting his cousin's power of attorney, Barfield sold their bank stocks, but instead of investing in farm mortgages as promised, he diverted the funds for personal gain, funneling them into worthless stocks. This scandal tarnished Barfield's reputation and highlighted the importance of trust and accountability in community leadership roles.

Other interesting lore linked with the Sanitarium took place between 1957 and 1959 when, during a class reunion for the Lake Geneva High School, an intriguing door prize was offered: a brick from the Oakwood Sanitarium. I would love to know where that brick is today!

Pranksters Turn to Oakwood Sanitarium:

As years rolled by, Oakwood Sanitarium morphed into local lore. Children dared each other to brave its crumbling corridors, weaving tales of ghosts and eerie hauntings that reverberated across town. For the bold—or perhaps reckless—youths of Lake Geneva, delving into Oakwood's decayed depths became a test of courage. Armed with only their bravery and a flickering flashlight, they plunged into the unknown, hungry to unearth its mysteries. Legends of concealed passages, abandoned chambers, and uncanny encounters fueled their fantasies, transforming each expedition into a thrilling journey of danger and discovery.

The lore surrounding Oakwood Sanitarium is rich with intriguing tales and curious anecdotes.

In 1935, rumors spread like wildfire after reports surfaced of a woman's arm discovered in a well shaft on the premises. Despite extensive searches, no such arm was ever found, but the story lingered in the city's collective memory for years.

Other incidents and pranks continued to add to the mystique of Oakwood. In later years, a wax dummy coated in catsup was placed in the basement, resembling a gruesome body. Police rushed to the scene, only to uncover the elaborate hoax. For years, the dummy was stored in the attic of city hall, a quirky relic of the past.

In September of 1937, a chilling headline gripped the readers of the Lake Geneva Regional News: "**Lake Geneva's 'Haunted House' Provides a New 'Murder' Mystery to Police**." The article recounted a macabre discovery prompted by a postcard from Chicago addressed to the Lake Geneva Police Department. The sender claimed that the head of a man, severed at the base of the neck, would be found on the main floor near the elevator shaft of the old asylum. Authorities rushed to the scene only to find a startling revelation upon closer inspection: the head was crafted from plaster of Paris, meticulously adorned to mimic realistic features, with red paint splattered across it to resemble blood.

In September of 1946, the peaceful evening air was shattered by the shrill sound of Fire Call No. 21 at 8:35 pm. Eager spectators, including volunteer firefighter Glydewell Gerber, rushed to Oakwood Sanitarium, affectionately dubbed the "Nut House." Racing four stories to the rooftop, Gerber discovered an oil flare left burning by pranksters, its deceptive glow mimicking a real fire against a nearby chimney. Though initially alarming, Gerber swiftly doused the harmless flare by nine o'clock, calming the relieved crowd as the fleeting excitement faded into memory.

Mario Del Rosso, in his book "Geneva Days," vividly recounts his escapades at the "Crazy House." In an excerpt, he describes how stepping into its open doorways felt like entering another world, where time seemed to stand still, and imagination reigned supreme. The eerie atmosphere of Oakwood left an enduring mark on all who dared to explore its mysterious depths.

Gary Gygax, a luminary in gaming culture, revealed in a 1991 Letter to the Editor featured in the Lake Geneva Regional News how his formative years at Oakwood left an indelible mark on his creative journey. He reflected on the exhilarating adventures within the "Crazy House," acknowledging how those experiences played a pivotal role in shaping the thrilling sense of excitement and danger found in the Dungeons & Dragons™ Game, a worldwide phenomenon. "However, besides drains, there were many service tunnels under the basement, passages for pipes and the like, and this maze stuck in my mind."

Gygax expressed a poignant lament for the absence of Oakwood, the once-standing, desolate, and forbidding structure, believing its presence could continue to ignite the imagination and curiosity of children in modern times. "In truth, my own adventures in the "Crazy House" on Oak Hill helped me to put together some of the sense of excitement and danger which millions have found in playing Dungeons & Dragons game."[7]

The End

The 1930 Census of Lake Geneva continued to record patients and staff associated with "The Lake Geneva Sanitariums," although the patients had been acquired by Dr. Warwick and relocated to the south shore of the lake near the Lake Geneva Club.

---

[7] The Lake Geneva Regional News Archive. (2001, March 1). Newspapers.com. https://www.newspapers.com/paper/the-lake-geneva-regional-news/19685/

Figure 33: Havenwood Apartments

Sadly, Oakwood Sanitarium met its demise in 1959 when it was demolished. The elusive surgery has not yet offered the information on its final usage and razing. The ruins of Oakwood's basement were finally excavated to accommodate the construction of Havenwood Apartments and Colonial View Condominiums in the 1970s.

Figure 34: St. Moritz

Lakeside Cottage became a hotel and clandestine Speakeasy during Prohibition. In 1926, it became the Lakeside Hotel & Restaurant. It was renamed the St. Moritz in 1942. In 2010, the "Redwood Cottage" was lovingly restored and decorated to represent the original style of a Gilded Age cottage. It is now the beautiful Historic Baker House. It is one of the few major wooden structures from that era to have survived destruction by fire or razing. A walk by it certainly sparks the imagination when you learn about its history!

Figure 35: Hotel Luzerne

Lakeside Sanitarium took on a new life under Joseph Finsky's ownership in March 1924, reopening as a hotel just two months later. In 1942, it was renamed the Hotel Luzerne. Demolished in 1975, it made way for the Hilton Inn, now known as Harbor Shores. Today, the lake views guests can see from the hotels are much the same as the patients would have had during their stays.

As the history of the Sanitariums of Lake Geneva fades into the vault of forgotten times, the legacy and profound impact they once had on Lake Geneva has been overlooked and lost.

Chapter 8: Oak Leigh Children's Sanitarium

While researching Dr. King's Lake Geneva Sanitariums, I stumbled upon another sanitarium in town. In operation for only 13 years, there was even less information available about this location than the "Surgery" building from the Oakwood Sanitarium campus.

I scoured the newspapers for more, and slowly, little snippets began to reveal details. Then, I made a trip to the DuPage County Historical Museum in Wheaton, Illinois, to view a private collection.

The Oak Leigh Sanitarium was established in August 1903 under the private supervision of Dr. Mary Eugenie Pogue, specifically catering to the treatment of children grappling with nervous diseases and mental afflictions.

Dr. Pogue, born in 1867 in Fond du Lac, Wisconsin, pursued her medical education in Chicago, Illinois, graduating from Hahnemann Medical College in 1900. She distinguished herself as a physician and was among the earliest child psychiatrists in Illinois.

Figure 36: Dr. Mary Eugenie Pogue

Dr. Pogue served as the Resident Physician at the "Illinois State Hospital and Colony for Feeble-Minded Children" in Lincoln, IL, for approximately two and a half years. She resigned from this position due to her declining health. By 1903, the population of the facility had surged to 1400 inmates, while the staff numbered fewer than thirty. Public institutions struggled to cope with the overwhelming demand, compounded by the prevailing stigma surrounding mental health and abnormalities, which often led families to conceal their loved ones away from society.

Figure 37: The Larsen Cottages, Oak Leigh Sanitarium

Friends of Dr. Pogue initially proposed the idea to establish a sanitarium, but the lack of funds posed a significant obstacle. However, when the idea was shelved, affluent parents of a needy child stepped forward to provide support. They assisted in furnishing two adjoining residences, enabling Dr. Pogue to assume control and establish the Oak Leigh Sanitarium.

The sanitarium had a progressive vision for its time, aiming to address the root causes of deficiency whenever possible. Its mission was to provide a nurturing environment for unfortunate children, focusing on attractive and hygienic surroundings. Additionally, the sanitarium sought to educate each child according to their abilities and prepare them for a life outside the institution rather than confining them indefinitely. Dr. Pogue's approach was reflective of empathetic and forward-thinking care and treatment of children with mental health challenges.

The Oak Leigh Sanitarium was strategically located near Geneva Lake, comprising three adjacent buildings nestled amidst acres of wooded land, with a barn included. This layout facilitated classifying patients into groups based on their mutual needs and benefits. By grouping patients according to their intelligence and habits, the sanitarium could tailor learning and liberties to suit each group appropriately.

Advertisements boasted of kindergarten, sloyd, medial and corrective gymnastics, the correction of speech defects, articulation, counting of beads and simple mathematics, modeling in clay, basket weaving, and the control and understanding of self. All these were to be taught, with each child receiving individual instruction. Sloyd or woodworking was considered valuable because it taught the accuracy of movement and was a desirable trade skill.

Education was carried out in the lower rooms of one of the buildings, with music and sewing taught in another one of the homes. At its peak, Oak Leigh Sanitarium had approximately thirty-five students varying in age from 2 to 30 years old who were cared for, as there was no age limit for the incoming "children."

The term "children" encompassed individuals ranging from 1 to 80 years old who resided with Dr. Pogue. Some school residents had been placed there as infants in the early 1900s and spent their entire lives within the institutions.

In addition, a private residence situated outside the campus provided boarding for sanitarium employees. Notably, the campus was conveniently positioned just two blocks away from the Lakeside and Lakeside Cottage facilities of the Lake Geneva Sanitariums, further enhancing its accessibility and potential for collaboration between the institutions.

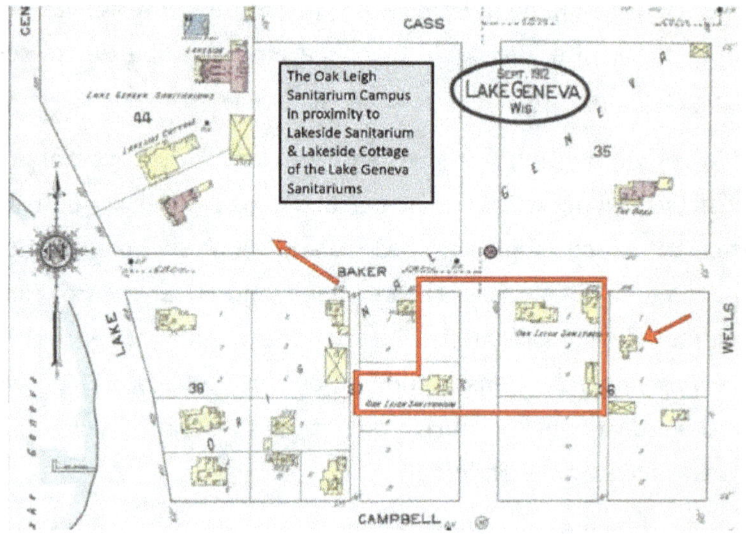

Figure 38: Sanborn-Perris Map, Lake Geneva, Walworth County, Wisconsin, September 1912

The involvement of Dr. William Stearns on the Consulting Board for Oak Leigh Sanitarium and as the Medical Superintendent of Lakeside Sanitarium reflects this.

Oak Leigh Educational Sanitarium
—FOR—
NERVOUS DISEASES IN CHILDREN
LAKE GENEVA, WISCONSIN.

DR. MARY E. POGUE
Physician in Charge
OAK LEIGH, LAKE GENEVA, WIS.
Long Distance Telephone
262 Lake Geneva

CHICAGO OFFICE:
1003-92 State Street
Hours 10 to 1 Saturdays
Wednesdays by Appointment
Telephone Central 4900

CONSULTING BOARD

Daniel R. Brower, M. D.
Walter S. Christopher, M. D.
Sanger Brown, M. D.
Homer V. Halburt, M. D.
Archibald Church, M. D.
William G. Stearns, M. D.

EDUCATIONAL EQUIPMENT
Motor and Sensory Training, Kindergartening, Sloyd, Articulation,
Speech Defects, Corrective and Respiratory Gymnastics,
Music, Raffia, Sewing, Modeling in Clay,
Reading, Writing, Mathematics,
Natural Science, etc.

OUR AIM is to prepare for lives of usefulness, children, who need to be educated privately. Trained Teachers and Trained Nurses.

Figure 39: Lake Geneva Sanitaria & Oak Leigh Advertisements

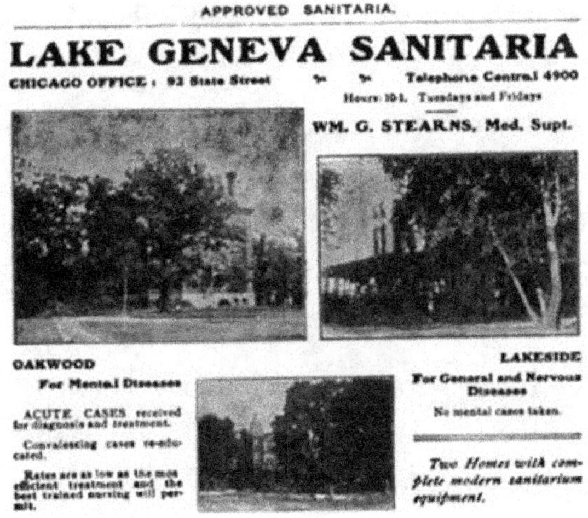

Figure 40: Lake Geneva Sanitaria & Oak Leigh Advertisements

A Closer Look at the Campus:

Figure 41: Oak Leigh Sanitarium Campus

403 Willow Street (now South Lakeshore Drive) - This served as the main building of the campus.

420 Baker Street - This was the secondary building of the campus, comprising the two Larsen Cottages.

414 Baker Street - This building was the residence of Anton and Anna Hylleberg. It offered boarding rooms, and in the 1910 census, six employees of the Sanitarium were listed as "Roomers." Unfortunately, it was demolished on August 27, 1986.

415 South Lake Shore Drive - Originally a barn, this building was later converted into a laundry facility and eventually transformed into a residence.

418 Willow Street (South Lakeshore Drive) - This was the third building added to the campus. However, it was demolished on July 27, 1977.

According to The Institutional Care of the Insane in the United States and Canada, Volume 3 from 1916, the estimated cost of buildings, property, equipment, and all was $60,000.[8]

Despite the financial investment in the institution, Oak Leigh Sanitarium prioritized the holistic well-being of its patients. Recreational activities were available to patients who could participate in games and sports and had assorted options for recreational activities. These included croquet, fishing, swimming, sledding, and ice skating. Additionally, some boys became members of the YMCA and joined sports teams. Those capable of doing so would assist with yard work and cultivating vegetables and flowers. Similarly, some girls would help care for their rooms and learn basic sewing skills as part of domestic science activities.

The 1905 Census indicates the presence of 12 "students" and 11 staff members at Oak Leigh Sanitarium. The staff titles included Physician, Teacher, Nurse, Gymnast, Cook, Gardener, and Laundress. Additionally, various want ads were placed for job opportunities at the sanitarium during this same time.

In the 1910 Census, the address of 410 Willow Street is listed, although it has not yet been verified. Rosena Housmann is recorded as the Head of Household, along with one roomer; they are both listed as sanitarium nurses. This is in addition to the 414 Baker St address, where Margaret Clarke is listed as a sanitarium nurse. The number of "students" has now increased to twenty, with a total of twelve staff members.

---

[8] The institutional care of the insane in the United States and Canada / by Henry M. Hurd [and others]. (n.d.). Welcome Collection. Retrieved April 22, 2024, from https://wellcomecollection.org/works/pstyd89y/items

Oak Leigh Educational Sanitarium appears to be thriving, with ongoing improvements to the campus and an increasing patient count. The community expresses satisfaction with the promising institution.

Dr. Pogue's involvement in the medical community is significant, as she actively participates in conventions, publishes papers, and delivers lectures. In her work, she emphasizes the importance of a private sanitarium setting, where there can be absolute control over the environment, diet, rest hours, work, play, and the company each child keeps. These factors are considered valuable for development. Dr. Pogue advocates for providing pupils with ample outdoor activities, a healthy diet rich in nitrogenous foods, and a meaningful quality of life, demonstrating her dedication to their well-being and holistic growth.

What happened next at such a progressive establishment was both shocking and disturbing. Three nurses devised a plan to kidnap a couple of brothers from the institution and hold them to collect unpaid salaries. Their scheme involved taking the two boys to East Troy and leaving them there with Nurse Mrs. Marie Souther. Miss Helen Flamm and Miss Helga Fredin, the other two nurses involved, returned to the sanitarium. One of them contacted the Chicago Tribune to accelerate the plan before retiring for the night.

On the morning of February 25, 1916, Miss Margaret Clarke, who was overseeing the facility while Dr. Pogue was at her home in Chicago, discovered that two children were missing. These children were Jerome and Walter Kalver, aged 10 and 12, respectively, from Lebanon, Indiana. As news of the kidnapping broke in the morning papers, Jacob Kalver, the children's father, saw the story. He immediately made phone calls to Dr. Pogue and the police, and reporters rushed to the scene by train to cover the unfolding story.

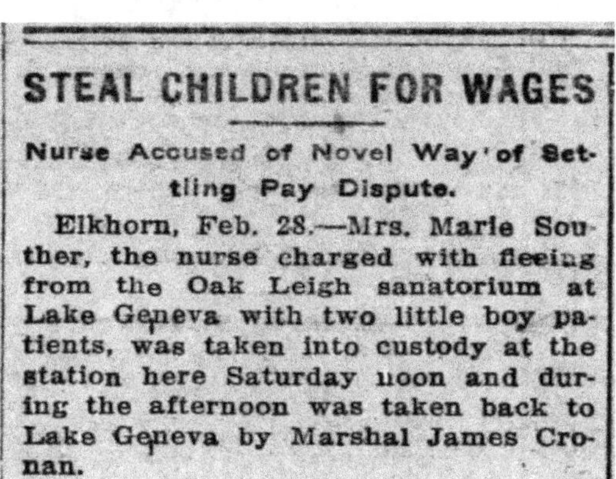

STEAL CHILDREN FOR WAGES

Nurse Accused of Novel Way of Settling Pay Dispute.

Elkhorn, Feb. 28.—Mrs. Marie Souther, the nurse charged with fleeing from the Oak Leigh sanatorium at Lake Geneva with two little boy patients, was taken into custody at the station here Saturday noon and during the afternoon was taken back to Lake Geneva by Marshal James Cronan.

Figure 42: Steal Children for Wages - Kenosha News 2.28.1916

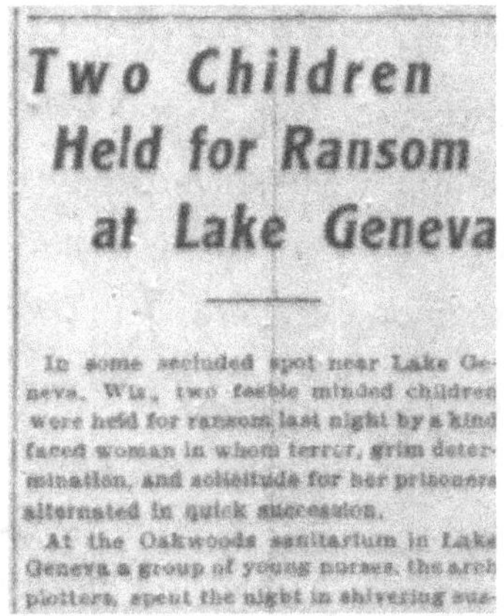

Two Children Held for Ransom at Lake Geneva

In some secluded spot near Lake Geneva, Wis., two feeble minded children were held for ransom last night by a kind faced woman in whom terror, grim determination, and solicitude for her prisoners alternated in quick succession.

At the Oakwoods sanitarium in Lake Geneva a group of young nurses, the arch plotters, spent the night in shivering sus-

Figure 43: Two Children Held for Ranson at Lake Geneva

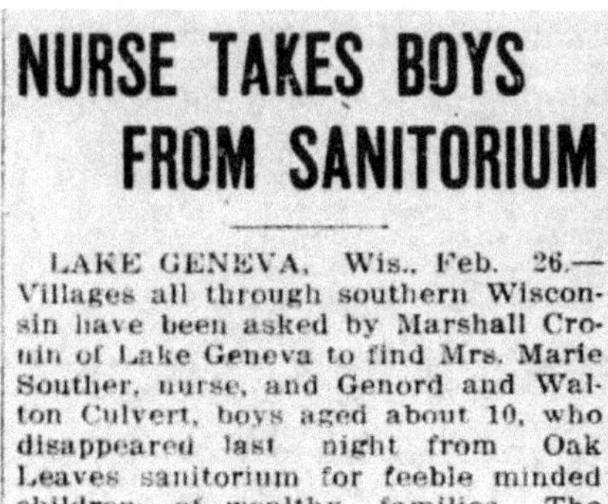

Figure 44: Nurses Take Boys from Sanitarium - Palladium 2.26.1916

Upon being notified by Lake Geneva Chief of Police James Cronin, Sheriff George Christie boarded a train from East Troy to Elkhorn. He saw Mrs. Souther and the children there and promptly took them into custody. Deputy Sheriff Ezra Button of Lake Geneva was assigned the responsibility of collecting Miss Fredin and Miss Flamm from the sanitarium with warrants.

After hours of frantic, long-distance phone calls to Chief Cronin and the Sanitarium, Mr. Kalver stated that he did not wish to prosecute, opting instead to take his children home. However, the legal troubles did not end there.

When asked if they would furnish $5,000 bonds each or go to jail, Miss Flamm replied, "Thank you, we'll all go to jail." She proceeded to claim that Dr. Pogue neglected to pay them, provided unsanitary living conditions, nearly starved them, and failed to have laundry done for the house or inmates. Miss Fredin and Mrs. Souther echoed these allegations, adding lurid details about the conditions at the Oak Leigh Educational Sanitarium.

One nurse even mentioned Beauty Pogue, the Dr.'s angora cat, which was said to have shed hair in the butter while strolling about the dining room table. It was revealed that they had originally planned to kidnap the cat, but the scheme had gone awry for undisclosed reasons. Consequently, the nurses spent the weekend in the county jail at Elkhorn until Attorney Charles Sumner could be present.

Dr. Pogue vehemently denied charges that the institution was unsanitary, attributing any disorganization to her relocation to a new location in Chicago. She claimed the nurses were doing spite work because they knew she was not bringing them to the new establishment.

Two ex-employees of the sanitarium, Miss Arlene Dahlander and Miss Edna Person, were also present and claimed that a total of $250 was owed to them, threatening to sue.

As a result of these mounting financial pressures, Dr. Pogue declared bankruptcy on Friday, March 24, 1916. Subsequently, on Saturday, April 29, a foreclosure sale of the property took place. The auction included a wide range of individual property, such as a fine library of standard works, a medical library, two pianos, and everything in the three houses occupied by Dr. Pogue's sanitarium.

This marked the demise of the Oak Leigh Sanitarium at Lake Geneva but not of Dr. Pogue herself. Today, the homes on campus all stand but one, and they are private residences.

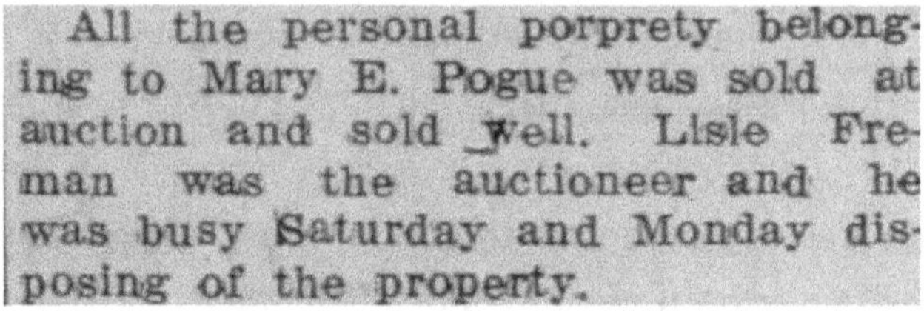

All the personal porprety belonging to Mary E. Pogue was sold at
auction and sold well. Lisle Fre-
man was the auctioneer and he
was busy Saturday and Monday dis-
posing of the property.

Figure 45: Ad About Mary E. Pogue's Properties

Unfortunately, the 1900 Calumet Ave. location in Chicago that Dr. Pogue was moving to, proved unsuitable and short-lived, adding further challenges to her situation. Seemingly bewildered, Dr. Pogue expressed her frustration, "The health department tells me the ordinance requires all doors to open outward, to have somewhat wider stairs, and requires fire escapes. In leasing this building, I specified that it was a sanitarium, but it seems that sanitariums come under the same restrictions as hospitals." Despite these challenges, she continued her search for a suitable location.

Eventually, the Mary E. Pogue School & Sanitarium was successfully established in Wheaton, Illinois, on a 25-acre rural estate. The campus comprised a main building called Pogue Manor, along with separate dormitories for girls and boys, a gymnasium, an education building, and a playground equipped with swings and slides. Additionally, a baseball diamond and tennis courts were available for recreational activities. Two of the buildings overlooked formal and vegetable gardens, with the latter supplying all the school's needs during the summer.

By the 1930s, Dr. Pogue faced financial difficulties and sold the school to U.S. Ayer. Upon his retirement, his daughter and son-in-law, Mr. and Mrs. MacGregor, acquired the school and continued its operations until its closure in 1966.

Nurse Margaret Clarke, who appeared on the 1910 census for Oak Leigh Sanitarium and first discovered the missing children, served as the Superintendent, as documented in the 25th Anniversary booklet of The Mary E. Pogue School & Sanitarium from 1929. Although her retirement date is unclear, she remained affiliated with the school as late as 1935, after Dr. Pogue's passing.

Dr. Pogue died on January 3, 1932, at Passavant Hospital in Chicago. For over 30 years, she championed and demonstrated a thought-provoking and compassionate understanding of exceptional children. Dr. Pogue was an educated, forward-thinking, and influential woman whose legacy in Lake Geneva has nearly faded into obscurity.

Chapter 9: Conclusion

From an old postcard to a journey full of curiosity and discovery, spanning over a decade and a half, this book sheds light on the forgotten stories hidden within the walls of the sanitariums.

In part, these stories were muted because the sites at which they took place now look much like the rest of Lake Geneva. In some cases, the sanitarium buildings are long-gone, and in others, they have evolved with time to reflect their modern usage. Uncovering the once-obscured stories and details within the historical record has rewarded me – and I hope, the readers of this book – with "old-time eyes," a lens for viewing the present while being mindful of the past. It's a depth-and-breadth perspective that has enriched my experience and shaped my attitude toward historic preservation in general and my appreciation of Lake Geneva in particular.

In tracing the evolution of Geneva Lake from its humble beginnings to its status as a luxurious retreat, we unveil a compelling narrative of transformation. From its origins, and as a sanctuary for escaped slaves to its status as a symbol of affluence and leisure, Lake Geneva's journey reflects broader changes in societal values and perceptions. Central to this narrative is the rise and fall of institutions like Oakwood Sanitarium, which pioneered innovative yet controversial treatments for mental health.

The story further unfolds with the establishment and eventual closure of Lakeside Sanitarium and Lakeside Cottage, offering insights into evolving notions of compassionate healthcare. At the heart of these institutions' narratives stands Dr. Oscar A. King, a figure whose original contributions to neurology and psychiatry permanently shaped the medical landscape.

However, the narrative isn't complete without delving into the saga of Oak Leigh Sanitarium, founded by Dr. Mary Pogue in 1903. Despite its noble mission to provide sympathetic care and education to children with mental health challenges, the institution faced unforeseen challenges, including a notorious incident involving the kidnapping of two brothers by disgruntled nurses. Despite these setbacks, Dr. Pogue's legacy persevered through establishing the Mary E. Pogue School & Sanitarium in Wheaton, Illinois, a testament to her enduring commitment to compassionate care.

These institutions, though now closed, remain pivotal in Lake Geneva's mental health care history, embodying a dedication to holistic treatment approaches. As we close the chapter on these storied halls and the memories they hold, let us carry forward the wisdom gleaned, and the tales uncovered. Let the enduring legacy of Oakwood Sanitarium, the Sanitariums of Lake Geneva, and Oak Leigh Sanitarium continue to resonate in the hearts and minds of future generations.

In commemorating this history, this book is intended as a timeless tribute to human resilience, the pursuit of medical progress, and the transformative power of compassion in the healing journey. Let us honor the legacy of the Sanitariums of Lake Geneva by continuing to strive for a world where compassion, understanding, and healing are accessible to all. May the spirit of Lake Geneva, with its rich history and enduring community, serve as a beacon of inspiration for generations to come.

References

1. History of Walworth County, Wisconsin" – Albert C. Beckwith 1912

Beckwith, A. C. (Albert C., & New York Public Library. (1912). History of Walworth County, Wisconsin. In Internet Archive. Indianapolis, Bowen. https://archive.org/details/historyofwalwort01beck/page/n5/mode/2up

2. Annals of Lake Geneva, Wisconsin" – James Simmons 1897

Simmons, J., & Harold B. Lee Library. (1897). Annals of Lake Geneva, Wisconsin, 1835-1897: an authentic account of the first discovery and settlement of the city of Lake Geneva and its vicinity and of its development, growth, and progress to the present time, with sketches of the lives of prominent early settlers. In Internet Archive. Lake Geneva, WI: The Herald. https://archive.org/stream/annalsoflakegene00simm/annalsoflakegene00simm_djvu.txt

3. Lake Geneva Newport of the West 1870-1920 Volume I" - Ann Wolfmeyer and Mary Burns Gage. 1976

Lake Geneva, Newport of the West | WorldCat.org. (n.d.). Search.worldcat.org. Retrieved May 2, 2024, from https://search.worldcat.org/title/lake-geneva-newport-of-the-west/oclc/3287443

4. Lovely Lake Geneva" - Eva Seymour Lundahl. 1950

National Register Of Historic Places Inventory—Nomination Form

https://npgallery.nps.gov/NRHP/GetAsset/NRHP/79000116_text

5. Mrs. Leslie Carter: A Biography of the Early Twentieth Century American Stage Star" – Craig Clinton 2006

Ford, J. L. (1902). Mrs. Leslie Carter in David Belasco's Du Barry: With Portraits of Mrs. Carter by John Cecil Clay, Together with Portrait of David Belasco, and Numerous Engravings of Photos. and Sketches in Black and White. In Google Books. F. A. Stokes.
https://books.google.com.pk/books/about/Mrs_Leslie_Carter_i n_David_Belasco_s_Du.html?id=yu0NAAAAYAAJ&redir_esc=y

6. The American Medical Directory. JAMA.

American Medical Association, & Gerstein - University of Toronto. (1906). American medical directory. In Internet Archive. Chicago, American Medical Association [etc.].
https://archive.org/details/americanmedicald01ameruoft

7. The Railway Surgical Journal – Volume 21, Issue 6

The National Association of Railway Surgeons: Official Report of the Sixth Annual Meeting held at Omaha, Nebraska May 31, June 1 and 2, 1893 by REED, R. Harvey (ed.): Good Hardcover (1893) | Attic Books (ABAC, ILAB). (n.d.). Www.abebooks.com. Retrieved May 2,

2024, from https://www.abebooks.com/National-Association-Railway-Surgeons-Official-Report/30520759539/bd

8. Polk's Medical Register and Directory – RL Polk and Co.

R.L. Polk, & McGill University Library. (1893). Polk's medical register and directory of North America. In Internet Archive. Detroit. https://archive.org/details/McGillLibrary-103413-266

9. Second Biennial Report of the State Charities and Reform of the State of Wisconsin for the Years 1885 and 1886.

Governor's message and accompanying documents Volume II 1887 - Full view - UWDC - UW-Madison Libraries. (n.d.). Search.library.wisc.edu. Retrieved May 2, 2024, from https://search.library.wisc.edu/digital/A7DEYVR3PWINLG9C/pages/AVYMOGE2AGZ5D48O?as=text&view=scroll

10. Chicago as a Medical Center – College of Physicians and Surgeons

Chicago College of Physicians and Surgeons. (n.d.). Lost-Colleges. Retrieved May 1, 2024, from https://www.lostcolleges.com/390-chicago-college-of-physicianew-page#:~:text=College%20of%20Physicians%20and%20Surgeons%20was%20founded%20by%20five%20Chicago

11. Medical and Dental Colleges of the West - Historical and Biographical - Chicago – 1896

Medical and dental colleges of the West: historical and biographical: Chicago | WorldCat.org. (n.d.). Search.worldcat.org. Retrieved May 2, 2024, from https://search.worldcat.org/title/7588058

12. Woman's Medical School, Northwestern University (Woman's Medical College of Chicago): the institution and its founders: class histories, 1870-1896

Woman's Medical School, Northwestern University: (Woman's Medical College of Chicago): the institution and its founders, class histories, 1870-1896 - Digital Collections - National Library of Medicine. (n.d.). Collections.nlm.nih.gov. Retrieved May 1, 2024, from https://collections.nlm.nih.gov/catalog/nlm:nlmuid-62810370R-bk

Maps:

1. Geneva from Walworth County Plat 1873

2. Bird's Eye View of Lake Geneva, Walworth Co., Wis. 1882. Drawn by Wellge & Poole. Beck & Pauli, lithographers, Milwaukee, Wis.

3. Plat Book of Walworth County Wisconsin 1891 – North West Publishing Company

4. Lake Geneva City Map – North – Walworth County Plat 1891

5. Lake Geneva, Walworth County, Wisconsin, Plat 1892 – Sanborn-Perris Map

6. Lake Geneva, Walworth County, Wisconsin, Plat 1900 – Sanborn Perris Map

7. Walworth County Land Information GIS

Websites:

1. Newspapers.com:

https://www.newspapers.com/

2. Ancestry.com:

https://www.ancestry.com/

3. Lake Geneva Regional News:

https://lakegenevanews.net/

4. Lake Geneva Public Library:

https://www.lakegeneva.lib.wi.us/

5. Geneva Lake Museum:

https://genevalakemuseum.org/

6. Walworth County Register of Deeds:

https://www.co.walworth.wi.us/203/Register-of-Deeds

7. Walworth County Historical Society:

https://www.walworthcountyhistory.com/

8. Wisconsin Historical Society:

https://www.wisconsinhistory.org/

9. Rock County Historical Society:

https://www.rchs.us/

10 Miami County Historical Society:

https://www.miamicountyhistory.org/

11. University of Illinois at Urbana-Champaign:

https://www.illinois.edu/

12. Wytheville Community College, Kegley Library:

https://www.wcc.vccs.edu/library

13. DuPage County Historical Museum:

https://dupagemuseum.org/

14. US National Library of Medicine:

https://www.nlm.nih.gov/

15. United States Federal Census (1860, 1870, 1880, 1900, 1910, 1920, 1930):

https://www.census.gov/

16. Wisconsin State Census:

https://www.wisconsinhistory.org/records/census

17. Oak Hill Cemetery, Janesville WI:

https://www.janesvillewi.gov/departments-services/public-works/oak-hill-cemetery

18. Find a Grave:

https://www.findagrave.com/

Miscellaneous Resource:

1. **Private Collection of Bill DeWitt**

2. **Oak Hill Cemetery, Lake Geneva, WI**

Newspaper Articles:

These are just a few stories about the sanitarium that can be found from coast to coast in the newspapers between 1885 and 1925.

The Lake Geneva Herald – Wisconsin

10.30.1885 - The Lake Geneva Herald shares that Charles Tallman shows no improvement in condition

3.12.1886 – The Lake Geneva Herald informs that Charles Tallman dies of General paralysis of the brain (paralytic dementia, or syphilitic paresis) at Oakwood Retreat

The Inter Ocean - Illinois

12.2.1887 – The Inter Ocean reports a preliminary step in the divorce case of Mr. Leslie Carter and Mrs. Caroline Louise Dudley Carter regarding the custody of their only child.

Hilo Daily Tribune – Hawaii

9.18.1897 – The Hilo Daily Tribune details how grief over the death of John Tallant's favorite son of 11 years of age, among other influences, caused his departure from the ordinary ways of life.

Marengo Beacon/Republican-News - Illinois

6.22.1888 - The Marengo Beacon/Republican-News contains a notice of Mrs. Fillmore being transferred from the sanitarium in Battle Creek, Michigan, to Oakwood Sanitarium at Geneva Lake.

The Sun – New York

4.24.1889 – The Sun details Dr. King telling of Mrs. Leslie Carter's delusions at Geneva Lake Sanitariums.

The Washington Critic – Washington D.C.

4.24.1889 - The Washington Critic story describes how Mrs. Carter saw snakes and heard knockings in her very nervous condition. Dr. King examined her in January of 1887 and pronounced her insane.

The St. Louis Globe-Democrat – Missouri

4.24.1889 – The St. Louis Globe-Democrat recounts that Mrs. Carter was confined for nine months under the care of Dr. Oscar A. King at Oakwood Retreat in Lake Geneva.

The Los Angeles Times - California

8.26.1897 – The Los Angeles Times reports the story of John D. Tallant, the San Francisco Banker, a raving maniac who threatened to shoot passengers on the train he was riding. Suffering from acute dementia, he was sent to Oakwood Sanitarium at Lake Geneva.

The Anaconda Standard - Montana

8.26.1897 – The Anaconda Standard story details the raving maniac banker John D. Tallant of California as insane on the train, throwing gold coins at passengers and drawing a revolver.

The Times – Washington, D.C.

8.27.1897 - The Times reports John Tallant's trouble as no more than nervous prostration.

San Francisco Chronicle

8.28.1897 – The San Francisco Chronicle details how Banker John Tallant suddenly was perfectly sane and in good health.

The Sacramento Union

9.1.1897 – The Sacramento Union reports that Tallant has entirely recovered from his mental derangement.

Lake Geneva Weekly News - Wisconsin

5.11.1893 - The Lake Geneva Weekly News contains an Editorial from the foreman of Geo L. Dunlap complaining of misconduct from wandering inmates on their grounds.

8.24.1893 - The Lake Geneva Weekly News reports that Judge Stitt, an inmate of Oakwood Retreat, wandered down to the lake shore and jumped in deliberately. He was rescued by C.M Baker.

The Chicago Tribune - Illinois

5.30.1901 – The Chicago Tribune runs the story of a lawsuit between brothers-in-law. William C. Dudley charges Amyas S. Northcote with malicious persecution and conspiracy with other persons to make his life a burden. A victim of alcohol and violently insane, Dudley was taken to Oakwood Sanitarium and detained for several weeks.

Kenosha News - Wisconsin

9.8.1903 – The Kenosha News reports on Charles Edward Shevlin, millionaire lumberman of Minneapolis, making an application for a writ of habeas corpus, requiring those who hold him in custody on the charge that he is insane to show cause why he should not be set free.

The Ottawa Journal – Ottawa, Ontario, Canada

9.19.1904 – The Ottawa Journal writes that the Superintendent of Insane Asylum says one-fifth of Chicago is insane.

Covina Argus - California

9.24.1904 – The Covina Argus reports on Dr. King and many other prominent authorities, stating that insanity rapidly increased.